A FEMINIST INTRODUCTION TO *Paul*

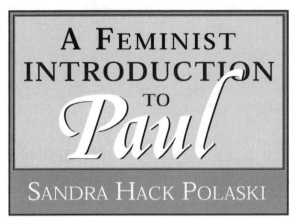

A FEMINIST INTRODUCTION TO *Paul*

SANDRA HACK POLASKI

CHALICE
PRESS

ST. LOUIS, MISSOURI

Biblical quotations, unless otherwise noted, are from the *New Revised Standard Version Bible*, copyright 1989, Division of Christian Education of the National Council of the Churches of Christ in the United States of America. Used by permission. All rights reserved.

Scripture marked NASB is taken from the *NEW AMERICAN STANDARD BIBLE®*, © Copyright The Lockman Foundation 1960, 1962, 1963, 1968, 1971, 1972, 1973, 1975, 1977. Used by permission.

Cover art: Mosaic of Paul, Notre Dame Church, Louviers, France; Photograph © Crosiers
Cover and interior design: Elizabeth Wright

This book is printed on acid-free, recycled paper.

Visit Chalice Press on the World Wide Web at www.chalicepress.com

10 9 8 7 6 5 4 3 2 1   05 06 07 08 09

Library of Congress Cataloging–in–Publication Data

Polaski, Sandra Hack, 1964-
  A feminist introduction to Paul / Sandra Hack Polaski.
    p. cm.
  Includes bibliographical references and index.
  ISBN 13: 978-0-827210-37-X (pbk. : alk. paper)
  ISBN 10: 0-827210-37-X
  1. Bible. N.T. Epistles of Paul—Theology. 2. Feminist theology. I. Title.
  BS2651.P54 2005
  227'.06'082—dc22

                                                      2004030143

Printed in the United States of America

FOR HANNAH

Contents

Acknowledgments

It was toward the beginning of a Society of Biblical Literature regional meeting, some years ago, that Jon Berquist, then of Chalice Press, said to me, "You know, someone needs to write a feminist introduction to Paul." The idea immediately took root in my imagination, and before the weekend was over, I sought Jon out and told him, "I think I'd like to be the person who writes that book." Too many years have come and gone from that day to this one; I deeply appreciate Jon's patience, perseverance, and encouragement, as well as the assistance and encouragement of Trent Butler in this book's final stages.

Numerous students, colleagues, and church groups have listened and asked insightful questions as I developed these ideas, often little realizing that the very process of dialogue helped me to clarify what I thought on various topics. I appreciate the opportunities to present my work, and the comments and discussions that moved me further along.

I appreciate those who have given me gifts of their time and attention in reading portions of this manuscript, particularly Judy Bledsoe Bailey, Sandy Rogers, and Richard Vinson. Their insights have contributed immensely to the quality of the completed project.

The Wabash Center for Teaching and Learning in Theology and Religion generously provided a grant for research in the early stages of this project.

The person whose voice (although not with the warm Charleston accent) speaks unacknowledged most often in these pages is undoubtedly my college New Testament professor, Edgar McKnight. From him I learned ways of approaching the New Testament texts that have become unalterably part of my own ways of thinking. Other teachers and colleagues will hear snatches of their own voices here as well; I hope I have not done violence to their viewpoints, even as I have made their ideas my own.

A number of congregations nurtured my faith, along with my inquiring mind. Especially formative were the people and programs of Woman's Missionary Union, where I learned to expect God to speak to *me* through the biblical texts.

Family and friends have not only listened to my work but helped me see beyond it. Special thanks are due to my husband Don, most honest reader, best colleague, and truest friend. Baby Will graciously waited to be born until the manuscript was in the mail—giving particular urgency to my reflections on new creation as the process of anticipating birth.

This book is dedicated to my daughter, Hannah Catherine Polaski, without whom it might have been finished sooner—but without whom I would have had much less reason to write it.

Abbreviations

JAAR	Journal of the American Academy of Religion
JBL	Journal of Biblical Literature
JSNT	Journal for the Study of the New Testament
JSOTSup	Journal for the Study of the Old Testament Supplement Series
NTS	New Testament Studies

INTRODUCTION

Paul and the Female Reader

"You know, the women in my church don't much like Paul." These were the first words one of my (male) doctor of ministry students uttered when I asked them why they had chosen my class on "Teaching and Preaching Paul." It's a sentiment that I've heard in various times and places, from laity and seminary students. I'm very much aware of this sentiment when I face all-male classes in Pauline theology. What is it about Paul's letters that women find so disinviting? Is it just that the letters have been chauvinistically interpreted by a patriarchal tradition? Or is the person whose literary identity stands behind them really a thoroughgoing misogynist? And what is it about the texts that conveys these often subtle but strongly sensed disincentives to women? Do women who read the Pauline texts have to choose between reading them as scripture and reading them as women? This introduction seeks to explore these questions and point to some strategies for women to use in reading Paul.

Reading Paul as Women

What are the interpretive options for women who read the Pauline texts? A number of feminist theologians and biblical scholars have addressed this question as it concerns the Bible in general. Rosemary Radford Ruether's groundbreaking *Sexism and God-Talk* outlines liberal, socialist, and radical

1

strains of feminism and seeks to integrate them into a feminist vision of society that avoids the weaknesses of each approach taken separately.[1]

Ruether's theologically informed social theory figures prominently in the work of a number of feminist biblical scholars, each of whom sketches a slightly different schema of possible approaches to the text. Katherine Doob Sakenfeld, for example, argues that the beginning point for all feminist readers of the Bible is a stance of radical suspicion. Her approach identifies three emphases or strategies with which feminists approach biblical texts:

1. finding texts about women to counteract texts "against" women;
2. finding in the Bible generally a critique of patriarchy or patriarchal structures; and
3. using texts about women "to learn from the intersection of history and stories of ancient and modern women living in patriarchal cultures."[2]

I am not primarily interested in judging Ruether's, Sakenfeld's, or another of these schemas as better, more complete, or more functional than are others. I am also not ready to insist that my own schema is superior, but I would like to consider the range of female readers' possible responses to Paul under four headings: *conformist, resistant, rejectionist,* and *transformational.*

Conformist Readings

Conformist readings of Paul are grounded in a high valuation of the biblical text as authoritative. This type of reading, as Carolyn Osiek has pointed out (she refers to it as a "loyalist" hermeneutic), claims that oppression must necessarily lie with the sinful interpreter rather than the good text.[3] The Bible proclaims a divine plan that is good for human beings, both male and female. Humans seek to follow their own plan rather than the one divinely provided for them, thus creating conditions of oppression and exclusion.

This approach, espoused by some evangelical feminists, may find little favor with less conservative Christian feminists. Some texts, after all, particularly some of those connected with Paul's name, seem to be oppressive and exclusionary no matter how they are read. Yet we can learn something from the work of evangelical feminists and others who take a conformist approach. Their readings are often careful and creative, since the options to reject the tradition or to condemn it as nonauthoritative have been set aside. At the very best, conformist readings of Paul represent the range of possibilities the texts allow without questioning the standing of the texts themselves.

Rejectionist Readings

On the other end of the spectrum stand *rejectionist* readings of the Pauline texts. Mary Ann Tolbert comments that, even for interpreters like herself with "a bias in favor of the Bible," a truly feminist stance demands that "this favorable inclination toward the Bible must be open to judgment and, if necessary, dismissal."[4] The rejectionist position is one that has deemed this "dismissal" necessary, for the Bible in general or for specific texts. Some of those who reject the Pauline texts do so in favor of a Jesus whom they see as more favorable to women. This is the *de facto* stance of many laywomen in churches. Such women would simply say that they "don't like Paul." Others have a more carefully considered position. They may reach this conclusion based on a study of texts in which Paul ignores women or subordinates women. Or, noting how women's activity and authority is circumscribed in the biblical texts, they may assume that everything not so described is exclusively male domain.

For some, of course, the rejection of the Pauline texts is part and parcel of the rejection of the Christian tradition as a whole, so that they define themselves as post-Christian. Again, even those who do not choose this option may well find that the rejectionists' critiques of the Pauline texts continue to challenge them, to push them to address the hard issues and the thorny passages that they might otherwise prefer to overlook.

Resistant Readings

Between conformist and rejectionist readings, and chronologically between them in the experience of some women who read Paul, is a *resistant* stance toward the text. While it may not delineate final conclusions regarding the text's authority or lack of authority, this stance questions the text's point of view and truth claims. It is the hermeneutic of suspicion. Resistant readings of Paul may follow any of the strategies outlined by Sakenfeld (see above). They may focus primarily on the women in Paul's texts, both the real women he names and the instances where the texts mention women, and ask how Paul's perspectives on women reveal his perceptions and biases. They may follow some of the outlines of what Osiek calls a "revisionist" perspective, seeking to bring neglected information into the tradition to correct the lacunae that create bias in the historical sources.[5] Those feminist readers who resist Paul's texts as they stand, and seek additional information to make his words more comprehensible, contribute valuable perspectives to the understanding of the texts. While their work often does not lead to simple conclusions, it enriches and complicates the total picture, making it less possible to argue for univocal interpretations.

Yet it is sometimes easy, in a resistant stance toward the text, to focus only on parts of the text and fail to comprehend the total picture. Those who select all the texts that specifically speak of women, for example, may lack what Sakenfeld calls a "principle of discernment [that] decides which set of texts is authoritative,"[6] so that texts that are positive toward women and those that are negative are simply tossed in together. A resistant stance may be particularly generative for research and exegesis, but it may not be finally satisfying for feminist interpreters.

Transformational Readings

Such interpreters—in particular, those who function and expect to continue to function within the Christian tradition with some notion of biblical authority—may need to seek *transformational* readings of the Pauline texts. These readings build on the insights discovered and challenges posed by the other three approaches to the text. They draw on Ruether's liberation-hermeneutical theological stance, with commitments to egalitarianism, a just society, and deeper human values.[7] Such readings will need to avoid the easy equation of what is authoritative with whatever is liberating, a caution frequently voiced concerning liberationist perspectives.

Yet the prophetic stance Paul frequently takes in his letters lends itself quite well to a perspective that takes the prophetic angle seriously. This stance seeks not merely the directives found within the text but also the directions that the text points. This stance also identifies the new paths the text blazes and is able to pursue those lines of thinking further than the text itself goes. What if, for example, we read Paul's letters for the radical equality he posits between Jew and Gentile and then argued that the theological *trajectory* of the text points toward a similarly radical equality between slave and free and between male and female? This sort of reading is bold and risky. It recognizes the seams and tensions within the text and digs in precisely at the points of tension, calling the text to witness against itself, when necessary, to expose the underlying assumptions of the text and make them available for evaluation.

At the same time, a transformational reading, such as I propose, must not seek to obscure the fact that it is an interested reading, committed to feminist principles. It will, though, insist on the acknowledgment that all readings are interested readings, built on particular commitments. By making clear its own presuppositions, a transformational reading will encourage interpreters to recognize the presuppositions of any reading. As I imagine it, a transformational reading will be broadly literary in character, with a focus on reader-oriented approaches to the text, attentive to structuralist, poststructuralist, and rhetorical-critical questions. Yet a transformational reading is not to be equated with any single approach to the text, any more than conformist, rejectionist, or resistant readings are. Rather, transformation requires attention to the texts as they stand, imagination to ask new questions of the texts, and creativity to shape critical approaches adequate to explore these questions.

What Might a Feminist Reading of Paul Do?

In a review, several years back, of Mieke Bal's *Lethal Love* and of Meir Sternberg's *Poetics of Biblical Narrative*, Daniel Boyarin makes a helpful distinction. He compares "a *thematic feminism*, which seeks to restore the woman's voice or critique the woman's suppression within the texts of male literary culture, and what might be called a *strategic feminism*, which seeks a different understanding of reading altogether from the one that patriarchy has promoted."[8] He identifies both, as well as the tension between them, as foundational to feminist literary theory. Along the way, Boyarin offers a number of observations about feminism and feminist hermeneutics that I find particularly helpful for describing avenues of approach that feminist readers of Paul have followed. These emphases are not mutually exclusive. Highlighting each in turn, though, helps one think through the various ways that feminist interpreters have attended to Paul's letters.

Make Visible the Invisible or Obscured Women

A feminist reading will seek to make visible the invisible or obscured women in the text. This means, obviously, that a feminist reading will pay close attention to Paul's actual references to women. It will identify female names and ask about Paul's female co-workers and female leaders in the churches Paul founded. It will examine Paul's directives to women and seek to reconstruct the historical situation into which Paul made his pronouncements. It will examine Paul's use of specifically female metaphors, such as childbirth (Gal. 4:19) and nursing (1 Cor. 3:2). It will inquire into ancient constructions of "masculinity" and "femininity" and investigate how Paul conforms to or digresses from those constructed gender identities (as in the "foolish" emotionalism of 2 Corinthians). It will ask about the real, historical, female readers/hearers of Paul's letters, whom he frequently overlooks in his rhetoric, and will seek to reconstruct how they might have understood his teachings and directives. But such a reading will also look for the women who are *hidden* in the text. As Boyarin notes regarding Bal's work, it will read "for the female subject-positions within" the texts it treats, and will show "how the reception history of the text has closed off subject-positions and ideological voices within the text."[9]

Perhaps the clearest example of this type of feminist reading is Antoinette Clark Wire's *The Corinthian Women Prophets*. Using the tools of rhetorical analysis, Wire shows not only what ideas Paul wants his audience to adopt, but also how he seeks to discredit or disarm his opponents. Her next step is to take seriously these opponents and their theology. Wire proposes that Paul's rivals for leadership in the Corinthian church were, in fact, a group of prophetically gifted women. They shared Paul's theology of Christ crucified and resurrected but understood the implications of Christ's resurrection quite differently than did Paul. They rejected their previous place in patriarchal family structures and claimed the right to speak to and for God. Paul denies these women their particular transformative reading of God's act in Christ, urging them toward a model of self-sacrifice that results in a more socially conservative set of behaviors. Since only Paul's side of the debate has survived, Wire argues, we posit these women's existence only through evaluating his rhetoric.[10]

Other volumes present sets of focused essays that provide both significant background material on the lives of first-century women and important commentary on how those women and their communities were shaped by Paul's leadership and influence. Kraemer and D'Angelo's *Women & Christian Origins* includes three articles specifically on Paul and the Pauline tradition, written by Margaret Y. MacDonald and Elizabeth Castelli. MacDonald's first essay, in particular, focuses on finding the "real women" in the undisputed Pauline texts. She argues that in the Pauline mission "women's leadership was neither different nor diminished in relation to that of men."[11] Work on the lives of ancient women, such as Ross Kraemer's *Maenads, Martyrs, Matrons, Monastics*[12] and Bernadette Brooten's *Women Leaders in the Ancient Synagogue*,[13] offer important context for the understanding of the women in Pauline communities.

Challenge the Accepted Reading

A feminist reading will also challenge the accepted reading, undermining its authority by suggesting that the text is not univocal. Such challenges may come from a range of perspectives: feminists who embrace a liberation-hermeneutical stance, evangelical feminists, and feminists who reject the texts' authority altogether. At first glance, so many different readings may seem to weaken the persuasive force of any particular reading. However, a plurality of readings accomplishes the more important goal of undermining, as Boyarin says, "the phallacy of mastery over the text which is the patriarchal and sexist gesture."[14]

Elisabeth Schüssler Fiorenza's groundbreaking feminist study of Christian origins, *In Memory of Her*, is best known for establishing a feminist critical hermeneutic that seeks to recover a "discipleship of equals" in the community around Jesus. In this book, originally published in 1983,

Schüssler Fiorenza also turns her attention to Galatians 3:28 and the household codes. Her extended and careful exegesis of Galatians 3:28 challenges other contemporary interpretations and concludes:

> Galatians 3:28 not only advocates the abolition of religious-cultural divisions and of the domination and exploitation wrought by institutional slavery but also of domination based on sexual divisions. It repeats with different categories and words that within the Christian community no structures of dominance can be tolerated. Galatians 3:28 is, therefore, best understood as a communal Christian self-definition rather than a statement about the baptized individual. It proclaims that in the Christian community all distinctions of religion, race, class, nationality, and gender are insignificant. All the baptized are equal; they are one in Christ. Thus, taken at face value, the baptismal declaration of Galatians 3:28 does not express "excessive enthusiasm" or a "gnosticizing" devaluation of procreative capacities.[15]

Schüssler Fiorenza not only challenges other readings of the Pauline texts, but she also highlights the tensions in the texts themselves. Regarding 1 Corinthians 7, Schüssler Fiorenza notes the liberating effect of Paul's permission for women to live a marriage-free life. At the same time she comments on his assertions (7:32–34) that those who marry have divided loyalties, "One can only wonder how Paul could have made such a theological point when he had Prisca as his friend and knew other missionary couples who were living examples that his theology was wrong."[16] In general, Schüssler Fiorenza credits Paul with holding a theological position that affirms the equality and giftedness of women and men in the Christian community. With his strong concern for order, though, as well as his clear preference for the marriage-free state, he introduces restrictions on women *as women* that do not function in the same way for men.

In addition to her own writing, Schüssler Fiorenza has encouraged other feminist interpreters to challenge accepted readings by coediting a collection of such essays, *Searching the Scriptures, Volume Two: A Feminist Commentary.*[17] The essays in this volume represent a wide variety of approaches. They are distinguished by their clear avowal of feminist perspectives and techniques. The collection is notable for its rejection of canonical boundaries or limits on interpretation. The Pauline tradition is represented in eleven essays (one book per essay, with the pastorals grouped together) in a section with the other epistolary literature of the New Testament. Beginning with Antoinette Wire's article on 1 Corinthians, these studies continue the practice of paying close attention to Paul's rhetoric in the letters and of refusing to assume, as Shelly Matthews aptly puts it, that "Paul is an oracle combating egomaniacs, hucksters, and interlopers."[18] Rather, the essays take Paul's opponents' point of view as seriously as Paul's own, particularly when it appears that Paul is attempting to limit manifestations of the Spirit that result in a reshuffling of the patriarchal social order. Furthermore, the essays (notably Elizabeth Castelli's on Romans) pay as much attention to the places women are *not* explicitly mentioned as the places that they *are*, raising questions of women's invisibility and the texts' ideology. Too, the placing of the New Testament epistolary literature (as well as the gospels and Revelation) in the context of other discourses that did not gain canonical status offers a different perspective on this literature.

Other one-volume commentaries also demonstrate, in the familiar book-by-book format, the difference that feminist reading makes. The *Women's Bible Commentary*, edited by Carol Newsom and Sharon Ringe and first published in 1992, contains separate articles on each of the NT letters by Paul or in the Pauline tradition. These articles emphasize the texts where women are mentioned or female figures are used metaphorically. The article on 1 Corinthians, for example, focuses largely on chapters 7, 11, and 14. Still, in each instance the specific references to women or female characters are set into the larger context of Paul's message in the letter and in the historical and social contexts in which it was written. A similar work from a more conservative theological viewpoint is *The IVP Women's Bible Commentary*.[19] In addition to articles on every book of the Protestant canon, it includes a significant number of short supplementary articles on topics such as "Women as Leaders," "Hierarchalism and Equality in the Home," and "Paul's Greetings to Female Colleagues." These are apparently intended to reinforce the validity of women's giftedness and leadership in the church today within a segment of Christianity in which women's leadership is still very much in doubt.

Uncover the Ideologies

Finally, a feminist reading will seek to uncover the ideologies underlying the texts, and, where possible, to reveal as well the counterideologies the texts incompletely suppress. An ideologically motivated reading cannot, of course, itself stand outside ideology. By foregrounding the question of ideology, it disarms ideology's power to short-circuit discussion and makes possible the investigation of the directions in which a text may be seen to point. Moreover, it will recognize that "ideology" is itself not a fixed notion but an ever-changing interplay of networks of power, both within the text and in the circumstances in which every interpretation takes place.

Elizabeth Castelli's work often focuses on questions of ideology, in her articles in *Searching the Scriptures* and *Women and Christian Origins* as well as her *Imitating Paul: A Discourse of Power.*[20] Castelli investigates Paul's calls for mimesis, or imitation, in his letters, particularly Philippians, and concludes that Paul presents an unreachable goal for his readers' imitation. In this way Paul reinforces his own position as the sole unquestionable authority and quashes expressions of difference (including gender difference) from his privileged role model. Castelli's work also represents feminist studies of Paul that do not engage primarily with texts in which Paul speaks specifically about women. Rather, Castelli argues that Paul's inimical attitude toward any expression of difference creates a hostile environment for women and others who embody or express some sort of social or theological "difference." All receive the subtle but clear message that their perspectives are not welcome in the community that looks to Paul for leadership.

Ideology is central in Elisabeth Schüssler Fiorenza's *Rhetoric and Ethic* as well. In this book she lets Pauline texts and Pauline discourse serve as the examples of her rhetorical-critical method. She focuses on awareness of the "politics of meaning" present in the texts and on the ethical implications of interpretation. This approach to the texts understands them to be neither simple statements of fact nor objective reports of conversation. They are rhetorically crafted and charged documents, engaged in political strategies of identification and "othering." As these texts and their rhetorical contexts are queried for their truth-claims, we as interpreters have the responsibility to evaluate these claims, the social relationships they make possible or impossible, the power networks they validate or exclude. Ultimately, Schüssler Fiorenza argues, we choose between competing readings based on a number of criteria, including plausibility, integrity, and our underlying convictions regarding the sorts of power networks that are appropriate in a just society.

Setting an Agenda

In short, then, the feminist reading of Paul I propose builds on the foundations established by previous scholarship. It will read, emphasize, or reinterpret overlooked, neglected, misintegrated, or differently interpreted Pauline texts. It will acknowledge, indeed celebrate, its own situatedness and the fact that it is not only just one possible reading, but also just one possible feminist reading. It will make as clear as possible how, why, and in what ways it ascribes authority to the text, how that authority works, and why that authority is necessary to the reader or reading. And it will seek to deal with the prophetic nature of the texts by reading for their trajectories. An ambitious project? No doubt! But my feminist commitments and my interest in the Pauline texts keep driving me in this direction.

The Ethics of Reading Paul

I admit, at the outset, to a bias in favor of the Pauline texts. Paul's letters, and the letters attributed to him, form a major part of the New Testament, which, together with the Old Testament, my religious tradition has typically claimed as "sole authority for faith and practice." They are the texts in whose words I learned to express my own most deeply felt spiritual ideas. Moreover, those texts generally agreed to have been written by Paul are both the earliest texts of the New Testament and the only ones for which we have a good deal of confidence about the author. I cannot help but think that exorcising Paul from my canon would make my religion a different religion and me a different person.

On the other hand, it is not merely a commitment to academic objectivity that leads me genuinely to hold open the option of rejecting the Pauline texts. They seem to come bundled with an androcentric worldview and a notion of textual authority (including, naturally, their own authority) to which I simply cannot consent. I cringe at the stories I hear of women and others who are emotionally, intellectually, and sometimes physically abused by persons who use these texts as warrant. I am aware, too, that the stories I hear do not begin to represent the scope and degree of abuse perpetuated under these texts' putative authority.[21]

It is, in a sense, *because* these texts have been (and continue to be) used abusively that I refuse to let them go without a fight. To give up, to admit that these texts are irretrievably gender-biased and patriarchal, would be to give bigotry the last word. It would consign all those who find words of comfort and redemption in these texts, and all those who live in communities that look to these texts for structure and guidance, to an existence that blindly replicates ancient understandings of the nature of male and female. The choice to read and interpret these texts is, at root, an ethical one. In my particular social and religious context the choice *not* to read these texts is an ethical decision too, with real consequences in the lives of the people among whom I live and work. So I choose to read, to struggle, and to seek the word of liberation and hope.

This is not to say that the task of reading Paul is an easy one. I often find Paul to be a human being whom I probably would not like if I were to meet him in person. He is often cocky, self-serving, and manipulative. These personal qualities persist even when he delivers a message of cooperation and self-sacrifice, using himself as a model. He is so certain that he is always right that he does not exercise due care in the formulation of his statements—even though he is aware that his obtuseness and self-contradiction give rise to confusion on the part of his hearers or correspondents (e.g., 2 Cor. 2:4; 7:8). A fuller understanding of the patterns of thought common in his era offers me some insight into his views, but oftentimes rouses little sympathy. He still makes me angry on a regular basis.

Ultimately, then, it is because I hold a notion of *scriptural* authority that I do not feel constrained always to take Paul's words at face value or to assume that his perspective and his intention in writing them should necessarily be the perspective and intention adopted wholesale by the reader. I value these texts because they are scripture, which is to say that they stand in a *living* tradition that entails a relationship between God and God's people. Thus my interest is in the *trajectories* present in the Pauline texts. I look not so much to see where they (and their author and first recipients) *stand*. I look to see where the texts *point*! Following along that line from their original first-century setting to our own day, I would argue, is the way to deal faithfully, as well as ethically, with the ancient texts we hold as scripture. I will seek to employ this practice as we explore the letters of Paul.

CHAPTER 1

Paul the Man

David J. A. Clines begins his essay "Paul the Invisible Man" with this thought-provoking statement:

> I know that most of the books about Paul are about his thought and that Paul as a human being is somewhere on the fringes, but you would have thought that someone somewhere would have found it interesting—I mean, *really* interesting for the understanding of his thought—that Paul is not just a Jew, a Pharisee, a scholar, a thinker, a traveller, an author—but also a *man*.[1]

For feminist readers in particular, Clines's point is well taken. Being a man, in any cultural and religious context, is *not* the same as being a human being. Especially for those of us who want to ask questions about the social and religious construction of gender, it is appropriate to begin by investigating how gender—specifically, his own masculinity—is constructed for our source, Paul himself. Clines's essay, which builds on his studies of the masculinity of other characters in the Hebrew Bible and New Testament, uses the evidence presented in both the undisputed and disputed Pauline letters to draw a portrait of Paul's male identity.

The First-Century Construction of Masculinity

Paul's masculinity, Clines argues, is socially constructed according to the expectations and social scripts of his first-century Mediterranean culture. Clines describes characteristics of masculinity that are inscribed over and over in the biblical texts, and appear, in his evaluation, in Paul's self-presentation as well: strength, violence, powerful and persuasive speech, male bonding, womanlessness, and binary thinking.[2]

For Paul, strength *is* manliness, as he urges in 1 Corinthians 16:13: *andrizesthe, krataiousthe*, literally, "be manly [the verb form of the noun *aner*, 'man, male'], be strong." Strength is important to Paul. Even when he knows himself to be "weak," he credits God with supplying him with strength (Phil. 4:13, 2 Cor. 12:10). While Paul distances himself from some sorts of violence (1 Cor. 4:21), the metaphors of battle and soldierly conduct, and even to a greater extent the metaphors of athletic competition, are a central part of his vocabulary of imagery. His embrace of these typically male competitive pursuits shows Paul to conform to this characteristic of masculinity as well.

Recent studies in rhetorical criticism have only served to add to the long-standing impression that Paul is an effective communicator, if more in his letters than in his physical presence (cf. 2 Cor. 10:10). While he eschews the notion that he is merely persuading, especially in 2 Corinthians, he understands his own words to convey divine power. Paul represents himself as womanless by his own choice (1 Cor. 9:5) and makes clear the warmth and depth of his personal and professional relationships with other males, particularly Timothy. Indeed, the fact that interpreters often overlook Paul's female co-workers may have to do with this very tendency in Paul's letters to value more highly his male relationships.

Finally, the prevalence of binary categories in Paul's thinking is well known: flesh and Spirit, law and grace, faith and works are just some of the important dichotomies in Paul's theological reflection. How these characteristics shape Paul's thinking and writing are worth our further consideration. One characteristic of Paul's expression, though, seems even more clearly a result of his maleness: his use of the fact of circumcision as a marker of Jewish identity and the lack of circumcision to indicate Gentile identity and freedom from the Jewish law.

Paul the Man and Male Circumcision

In Galatians 5:2, Paul addresses his readers: "Listen! I, Paul, am telling you that if you let yourselves be circumcised, Christ will be of no benefit to you." The comment may not be surprising in itself, since circumcision is one of the issues that underlie the letter. But the female reader who expects to find herself addressed in the words of scripture is suddenly confronted with a second person plural that categorically leaves her out. If the *hymin* ("you") and second person plural verb of Galatians 5:2 is not addressed to her, what about the *hemas* of the previous verse, "For freedom Christ has set *us* free"? What about the *hymeis* ("you") who are no longer male and female, but one in Christ Jesus (Gal. 3:28)? The corporate addressee of Paul's letter, "the churches of Galatia," does not seem to change; yet Paul writes as if that addressee were male and were considering for himself the possibility of circumcision.

Why is it, exactly, that Paul, himself a Jewish male "circumcised on the eighth day" (Phil. 3:5), is so adamant about prohibiting the ritual for the Galatian believers? If the presence or absence of a foreskin is really such a crucial religious issue, then the letter to the Galatians would seem far removed from the lives of believers today. For us circumcision is typically a medical, not a religious, decision. It is particularly far removed from the concerns of female readers, whose only likely experience with circumcision would be in the decision whether to have the procedure performed on an infant son.[3] ⌐As we will see, though, "circumcision" represents, for Paul, much more than the ritual itself. Rather, it stands for a way of living that Paul strenuously opposes, calling it "another gospel which is not another" (Gal. 1:6–7, author's translation). ⌐

To understand the nature of the Galatians debate, it is crucial to remember that what we today call "Christianity" was, in its earliest days, generally understood as yet another offshoot of the wide variety of first-century Judaism. Jesus was a Jew. His first followers were all Jewish. His ministry was, with a very few possible exceptions, carried out within the confines of Israel. The early church believed that their Messiah had come in the person of Jesus. Other Jews might have seen the church Jews as mistaken or wrong. Still, belief in Jesus would not, by itself, have made them something other than the Jews they had always been. Indeed, the depth of the antipathy of some Jews toward this new movement (as reflected, for example, in the book of Acts, and in Paul's testimony of his own former life) reflects the anger reserved for heretics rather than for unbelievers.

Nor would the conversion of the first few Gentiles to this movement have marked it as clearly outside the bounds of Judaism. While most branches of Judaism did not actively seek out converts, proselytism was not unknown. An even larger number of Gentile "God-fearers" lived particularly in the cities of the Roman Empire and respected the Jewish God. They worshiped with Jews in their synagogues, but without undergoing the entire process of conversion to Judaism. That process would have included, of course, circumcision for males who were previously uncircumcised. Again, other Jews might have suspected, or known, that the followers of Jesus were not strenuous in their demands of circumcision for Gentile converts. This would have made them lax or heretical Jews, not something other than Jews.

What Paul proclaims, on the other hand, is a new status, "in Christ," to which Jews come as Jews and Gentiles come as Gentiles.[4] Gentiles need not become Jews to be "in Christ." Indeed, Paul goes so far as to say that the very distinctions of Jew and Gentile cease to exist "in Christ" (Gal. 3:28).[5] What God has done in the death and resurrection of Jesus, Paul insists, is so monumental that it supercedes even the Law. The Jewish Torah, once seen as the good gift of God to the chosen people, is now viewed metaphorically as the caretaker for a minor child, no longer necessary when the child reaches adulthood (Gal. 3:23–25). Where Jews appeal to the Law given through Moses, Paul goes back further, to Abraham, and reads the promise to Abraham (Gen. 12:1–3) as fulfilled in Christ. The Abrahamic covenant is important to Paul for several reasons:

1. It is based on faith, which God imputes as righteousness (Gal. 3:6; cf. Gen. 15:6).
2. It refers specifically to the Gentiles, or "nations."
3. It clearly precedes the Mosaic Law, by 430 years in Paul's reckoning (Gal. 3:17).

Scripture itself, Paul proclaims, witnesses to the promise to all people, Gentile as well as Jew. That promise has been fulfilled in Christ.

But why is circumcision the symbol of the Law to which Paul appeals? One might argue that it is because circumcision is a literal, physical mark—and in Paul's context, a mark of religious identity. Yes, one can be baptized, but eventually the water of baptism dries off. One can take vows, but one can also repudiate them. When circumcision is socially coded as an identity marker, it remains as a visible sign and frequent reminder, particularly to the circumcised man himself, of his identity, in this case as a Jew, a member of the people of God.

Still, I would suggest that Paul's maleness is, at least in part, the explanation to a question that is obvious in the Pauline letters but rarely asked: Why is *circumcision*—and not some other characteristic of Jewish practice—the synecdoche of Law/Jewishness in Paul's letters? Why not, for example, kosher laws? Kosher regulations were a part of daily life for Jews. They involved not only the designation of which meat could be consumed (recall that most people ate meat only rarely), but also the segregation of meat from all dairy products, the maintenance of separate cooking utensils for meat and dairy, and (by standards of the time) sanitary food preparation procedures. Contemporary scholarship, while fragmentary, suggests that Jews in the diaspora did keep the kosher laws to the extent possible.[6] Furthermore, issues of kosher food seem to have been involved in the difficulty that some Jews experienced in accepting Gentiles as full members of the movement (Gal. 2:11–14; cf. Acts 10:9–16). Why, then, does Paul choose the one-time event of circumcision rather than the daily practice of kosher law to summarize Jewishness and the difference between Jews and Gentiles? I suspect that it is because, for Paul, as a male, his circumcised state reminded him regularly of his Jewishness, while the primary responsibility for keeping the various precepts of kosher laws, and the choice of whether to follow those laws, fell primarily to women in Paul's circle of acquaintances.[7] Paul speaks, as is typical for males of his day, as a man to men, and draws his imagery from male experience. Women readers or hearers are left to extrapolate for themselves what might be the analogous images or teachings.

The Problem of Language

It is worth commenting, too, on the language in which Paul wrote, particularly as issues of inclusive language and appropriate translation have become a hot topic in biblical interpretation. It is, admittedly, frequently difficult for native speakers of English to imagine the worldview that is called into being by a language so differently structured as Greek. In English, of course, gender is indicated only by singular personal pronouns, and generally follows natural gender (a biological male is "he," a female is "she," and a thing that does not have biological or natural gender is "it"). By contrast, in Greek every noun has a *grammatical* gender, masculine, feminine, or neuter, and grammatical gender may or may not reflect natural gender. Pronouns, both singular and plural, are likewise gendered, following the grammatical gender of the nouns to which they refer. Thus, as inclusive language proponents argue, it means something different, for example, to use a masculine personal pronoun for "God" in English than in Greek. In English grammatical gender implies natural gender and suggests that the antecedent of the pronoun is "male." In Greek the grammatical masculine does not necessarily imply that the antecedent is male.

On the other hand, the grammatically gendered structure of Greek often serves to make women even more invisible than do English language structures, particularly since the masculine plural is used when a group of men *and* women is in view. (When the group is impersonal, and particularly when the group includes items with different grammatical genders, the neuter plural pronoun is often employed.) The use of the masculine plural is observable both with pronouns and collective nouns. An example of the latter is the term *adelphoi*, "brothers," that Paul frequently uses. The NRSV often translates it as "brothers and sisters" when the reference seems to be general. The difficulty, of course, is that it is often impossible to know whether a grammatically masculine plural noun or pronoun refers to men only, or men and women together. The women are grammatically rendered invisible.

Thus both Paul's culturally constructed masculinity and the structures of the language in which he writes function to marginalize women. My reading of the letters suggests to me, however, that Paul does not specifically *exclude* women. Rather, they are *invisible* to him except when his attention turns toward what we might term "women's issues," that is, situations in which the different gender of women matters to his argument. Paul, not unlike other male writers from antiquity to the present time, writes as if the masculine gender, and indeed, the male body, is "normative." Women are addressed specifically only as they are different from that norm.

Male and Female in the First-Century World

In contemporary society, we are aware, at some level, that the definitions of appropriate male and female behavior are socially constructed and that those understandings are sometimes contested. For example, a public service campaign appearing on billboards in my area of the country seeks to curb violence against women. To do so, it offers an alternative message about masculinity: close-up shots of several young, "tough"-looking men and the slogan, "Our strength is not for hurting." Debates over gender roles or sexual orientation are similarly sites of contested understandings of what makes people male or female. Yet, as a culture, we are so strongly shaped by certain presuppositions regarding maleness and femaleness that it is often difficult for us to imagine our thinking being grounded otherwise. This is, then, precisely what we must do to understand how Paul and his contemporaries would have understood what it means to be male or female.

The One-Sex Model

Contemporary discourse about the human body and about human behavior that relates directly or indirectly to the body assumes that there are two sexes: male and female. To agree on two sexes does not, of course, necessarily lead to agreement on what the existence of the two sexes *means* for human beings and their relationships to one another. Are they related in an immutable hierarchy, either of strength (as in a traditional patriarchal social structure) or of refinement (as some early women's suffragists argued that the "finer" nature of woman could reform the political process)? Are they (at least theoretically) equal but utterly incommensurate (as in popular parlance, "men are from Mars, women are from Venus")? Or is there really no difference whatsoever between men and women except their sexual equipment, all other sexual and gender differences having been created and sustained by the workings of society? These and similar questions may continue to be debated, but note that they all rely on a notion that the human being exists, as it were, in two "varieties": male and female.

Theorists have termed this concept a "two-sex model." Such a model did not hold in antiquity (and, indeed, was developed only around the seventeenth and eighteenth centuries). Prior to this, as Thomas Laqueur has demonstrated, thinking regarding the body proceeded along what has been termed a "one-sex model," with only one kind of body—the male body—representing the epitome of human physical perfection.[8] Actual human bodies were perceived as existing on a kind of continuum from (male) perfection at one end—usually described as hot, dry, hard, strong, controlled, and the like—to the female at the other end, understood as cold, moist, soft, weak, unstable, and susceptible to various passions. Male and female bodies were not understood as having different *kinds* of sexual equipment. Rather, men (by virtue of more fortuitous conditions during conception and gestation) had their sexual organs on the outside of their bodies, whereas women's sexual organs were turned inwards, where conditions caused them to function differently than those of men.[9] Moreover, the "stuff" of which a woman's body was made was generally considered to be less perfectly developed than, and thus different from, the "stuff" of a man's body. This female "stuff" was "naturally" colder, moister, and so forth, well suited to the kinds of disciplines a woman needed in order to be able to function in society, but inappropriate to the kinds of work a man would undertake. A woman, then, was physically a lesser version of a man. Discussion of her physiological or spiritual status, then, proceeded from that fundamental assumption.

To describe human sexuality as existing on a continuum is not to suggest that the ancients perceived human beings as being equally distributed along that continuum. True androgynes were primarily the stuff of legend (although they were prominent in Greek and Roman legend and the art based on it). Nor was it seen as desirable for a woman to try to "improve" herself by taking on masculine characteristics. On the contrary, women who did so (whether described by their sexual behavior or other characteristics) were typically seen as "unnatural," if not downright monstrous. For a man, however, maintenance of his masculinity was a more or less active duty. Especially among the upper classes, a boy's upbringing would be designed from infancy onward to shape him, literally as well as figuratively, into the ideal of manhood. The nonelite of Paul's circle probably found it impossible to enlist the aid of countless nurses, trainers, and masseurs to shape the young. Still, parents, particularly the freeborn, would likely have been similarly interested in seeing their sons grow up to model masculine ideals.

Female Weakness

When Paul *does* take account of women separately, then, his understanding of the female body often requires that he make an exception for their innate weakness. As Dale Martin has noted, Paul's inability to challenge his society's dominant physiology of gender results in his dropping the strategy of status reversal that he typically deduces from the new life "in Christ":

> Throughout 1 Corinthians Paul attempts to undermine the hierarchical ideology of the body prevalent in Greco-Roman culture. He attempts to make the strong weak and the weak strong. He calls on Christians of higher status to please those of lower status. He insists that those who see themselves as spiritual modify their behavior, such as speaking in tongues in the assembly, to accommodate those they consider spiritual inferiors. Paul even implies that the higher-status Christians should follow his example and lower themselves socially to identify themselves with those of lower status.
>
> But when it comes to the male-female hierarchy, Paul abruptly renounces any status-questioning stance. Instead, he accepts and even ideologically reinforces a hierarchy of the body in which female is subordinated to male. The reason for this seeming inconsistency, I have argued, has to do with physiology. The "stuff" of female nature is differently constituted from that of male nature. Women's bodies are different from men's. This difference is not just in the way we today think of them as different, in that they have different "parts." The difference for Paul and for Greek thought in general lies in the very substance, the matter that makes up their bodies. The material "stuff" of women's bodies is seen as constitutionally different from that of men's.
>
> Until the resurrection, women's bodies will be different from men's, more porous, penetrable, weak, and defenseless. Even after the resurrection femininity will not be any less inferior. It will simply be subsumed into the superior strength and density of masculinity. Because of the ancient definitions of masculine and feminine,

therefore, "female" can never be equal to "male"—in spite of the fact (in Paul's language) that in the kingdom of God people who are now women will then be equal to people who are now men. Those who were formerly female will be equal, however, because their femininity will be swallowed up by masculinity. The inferior nature of their female stuff will be transcended as their bodies are raised to a higher level on the spectrum that extends from higher male to lower female. Strange though it may seem to modern Christians, Paul cannot consider the female equal to the male. For the present he cannot consider women equal to men due to the hierarchy of physiology.[10]

From such a starting point, we may be surprised not at how differently Paul represents men and women but how little he differentiates between them. Certainly the Hebrew understanding of both male and female as created in the divine image serves to moderate this notion of the imperfection of the woman. Still, to proceed from these assumptions regarding physiology is to come at the understanding of men's and women's roles in a very different way than we assume to be the case today.

Romans 1 and Homosexuality

Finally, considering how Paul's understanding of the meaning of male and female is different from that of his modern interpreters illuminates another thorny Pauline text. In Romans 1, Paul describes the idolatrous rejection of God as proceeding to sexual impurity:

> For the wrath of God is revealed from heaven against all ungodliness and wickedness of those who by their wickedness suppress the truth. For what can be known about God is plain to them, because God has shown it to them. Ever since the creation of the world his eternal power and divine nature, invisible though they are, have been understood and seen through the things he has made. So they are without excuse, for though they knew God, they did not honor him as God or give thanks to him, but they became futile in their thinking, and their senseless minds were darkened. Claiming to be wise, they became fools; and they exchanged the glory of the immortal God for images resembling a mortal human being or birds or four-footed animals or reptiles.
>
> Therefore God gave them up in the lusts of their hearts to impurity, to the degrading of their bodies among themselves, because they exchanged the truth about God for a lie and worshiped and served the creature rather than the Creator, who is blessed forever! Amen.

> For this reason God gave them up to degrading passions. Their women exchanged natural intercourse for unnatural, and in the same way also the men, giving up natural intercourse with women, were consumed with passion for one another. Men committed shameless acts with men and received in their own persons the due penalty for their error.
>
> And since they did not see fit to acknowledge God, God gave them up to a debased mind and to things that should not be done. They were filled with every kind of wickedness, evil, covetousness, malice. Full of envy, murder, strife, deceit, craftiness, they are gossips, slanderers, God-haters, insolent, haughty, boastful, inventors of evil, rebellious toward parents, foolish, faithless, heartless, ruthless. They know God's decree, that those who practice such things deserve to die—yet they not only do them but even applaud others who practice them. (Rom. 1:18–32)

Most modern interpreters read this text as Paul's condemnation of homosexuality and point to verse 26 as evidence that Paul is unusually comprehensive in his judgment, encompassing female as well as male same-sex behavior. Yet while it is clear that Paul condemns what he understands as improper sex and that he sees this behavior as stemming from idolatry, the direct equation with what we term "homosexuality" evidences a slippage that results from our different understanding of what constitutes sexual identity.

In several articles, Diana Swancutt has explicated how Romans 1 demonstrates ancient, rather than modern, ideas about sexuality.[11] She notes that ancient interpreters do not understand the reference to women's "exchanging natural intercourse for unnatural" (v. 27) as referring to female same-sex activity (at least not exclusively so). Indeed, the modern understanding of sexuality focuses on the identity of the object of the sex act. Thus men who have sex with men or women who have sex with women engage in "homosexual" relations. Ancients, however (including both Paul and his first interpreters), defined sexual identity by the nature of the sexual activity, either active or passive (or penetrator and penetrated). The proper and "natural" role for a man was the active role. The woman was supposed to be passive. Either a woman who took the initiative in sex (with another woman, a minor of either sex, or a man) or a man who chose the passive role was acting contrary to "nature."

Paul theologizes the argument and takes it one step further, Swancutt claims. He does this with his reference to the God-given *doxa*, "glory" (v. 23). This *doxa* is appropriate to men (since they have been divinely placed at the top of the sexual hierarchy), but forfeited by idolaters. Since idolatrous men reject God's *doxa*, God allows their *doxa*, their maleness, to slip, as they slide down the continuum from ideal maleness to softness and passivity, feminine characteristics that men should know to avoid. Some contemporary interpreters read Paul's "received in their own persons the due penalty for their error" (v. 27) as an eerily predictive warning regarding AIDS or other sexually transmitted disease. In so doing they get Paul's meaning partly right: the kind of sexual activity Paul describes does result in the changing or degradation of human bodies. But Paul does not refer to the downfall from a healthy body to a diseased one. Rather, he understands improper (i.e., insufficiently manly) sexual activity to result in a degraded body, one that is less male, that has lost the glory (*doxa*) granted by God to male bodies.

Again, female readers may be particularly aware that Paul characteristically speaks as if his readers or listeners were all male. He appeals to other males regarding the viewpoints and outlooks he assumes they share, in this instance, the value of what is culturally given as "manliness." It is manly (and instituted as such by God) to take the active role in sexual intercourse. Therefore, it is wrong for a man either to be passive (whether with a woman or with another man) or to cause another man to be passive— thus the particular emphasis on male-male intercourse as representing inappropriate and idolatrous behavior on the part of both partners. Also characteristically, Paul occasionally remembers that he has females in his audience, too. He reminds them that they have a "natural," God-given sex role as well (although perhaps the comment about women should be construed as also directed to Paul's male audience, shaming them for allowing women to be active in sexual relations with them).

Such a reading of Romans 1 demonstrates that use of this passage is problematic in contemporary discussions of homosexuality and sexual orientation. Indeed, by this reading, the "choice" of one's sexual partner is somewhat beside the point. How one comports oneself in the sexual act seems already to be determined by the practice or avoidance of idolatry and by whether one has thereby lost or retained the *doxa* ("glory" or "honor") appropriate to one's gender. Human glory or honor, Paul suggests, necessarily reflects divine glory. Those who forfeit God's glory by the practice of idolatry will necessarily also forfeit the honor appropriate to their human bodies and will act physically in ways that are not honorable, but rather shameful.

Paul's *example* of shameful physical acts is same-sex male intercourse (and, apparently, any sexual act in which a woman takes an active role). But he regards this behavior as the *symptom* and *result* of idolatry (with its accompanying loss of *doxa*). The main issue is the voluntary rejection of one's God-given maleness (the place of honor on the continuum of gender). Clearly, this way of framing the issue makes it difficult to use Paul's statements to obtain a clear "biblical perspective" on homosexuality as we understand it in our modern context. But the difficulty underscores the point. My primary aim is to demonstrate Paul's ways of understanding masculinity and femininity, ways very different from those we subscribe to today. Because Paul understands the "natural" state of maleness or femaleness differently than we do, it stands to reason that his ideas of the place and role of men and women will be different from ours as well.

A Women-Only Christianity?

Male leaders in the early Christian movement may, in fact, have reacted against the possibility that their faith might become a women-only movement. Such cults, made up either exclusively or overwhelmingly of women, were known in the ancient Greek and Roman world: the cult of Dionysus, for example, or that of Adonis.[12] Women seemed to flock particularly to the "new" or "foreign" religions as opposed to the traditional Greek and Roman deities. In the second century the pagan critic Celsus characterized Christianity as a religion that actively seeks and is able to acquire as converts "only the silly, and the mean, and the stupid, with women and children."[13] This comment and Origen's early third century rejoinder to it come from later than the Pauline period; still, they may point to the fact that Christianity from its earliest days, like other new religions, drew to its ranks more female than male adherents. While the frequent pairing of men and women in Luke-Acts strikes contemporary readers as a laudable instance of gender inclusivity, Mary Rose D'Angelo has suggested that the ancient author may well have had another purpose in mind. The biblical writer may have sought to demonstrate that men as well as women were involved in the Jesus movement, that the women involved were properly associated with men in culturally commendable ways, and that the men showed appropriately "manly" virtues.[14]

Paul, as a typical male of his time, then, may well have shared these misgivings and allowed them to shape his reactions to women's leadership in his churches. Like others in his society, Paul subscribed to the prevailing ideology that valued "men's activities" over "women's activities." He worried, not without cause, that a community in which women played too great a role would eventually lose its male membership. (A modern analogy might be the unease that grips some neighborhoods when families of color move in or when affordable housing is built.) On the other hand, Paul genuinely believed that women were valid members of the believing community (note, for example, how many women Paul names as fellow-believers and co-workers;

see below, chapter 2). He preached a gospel that emphasized themes of reversal (1 Cor. 1:18–31) and the value of every member (1 Cor. 12). The presence of these tensions gives us the opportunity to query more closely Paul's writings, in light of what we know of his probable social milieu, to see what we may find that encourages and supports women in the church today.

Paul's Metaphorical Language: A Space for Caveat?

Given all that we have considered about Paul the first-century male, it should strike us as more than a little surprising to find Paul, from time to time, representing himself metaphorically "in drag," imaging himself in a female role. For example, in Galatians 4:19, Paul comments that he is "in the pain of childbirth until Christ is formed in you." The metaphor is complicated because it does not follow logically. Paul has the labor pains, but Christ is formed in the Galatians. Too, the image of labor pains is sometimes used eschatologically as symbolic of the woes to come (cf. 1 Thess. 5:3; Mk. 13:8; Rev. 12:2). Nonetheless, it is notable that Paul chooses to apply this imagery to himself, apparently unconcerned that he is presenting himself in a "weak" and "body-focused" female role. As Carolyn Osiek comments, "Perhaps a man willing to use such an image is not as alienated from women's experience as Paul is often made out to be."[15]

Indeed, Beverly R. Gaventa argues that Paul quite intentionally utilizes the labor metaphor to link his apostolic vocation with apocalyptic expectation. Moreover, she claims, this text is an important theological link between Paul's personal appeal and the rest of the letter. Precisely at this critical juncture, Paul claims to be in the process of giving birth, reflecting the experience of all creation as it awaits God's fulfillment in Christ.[16] Gaventa asks whether this self-portrayal ought not lead us to reconsider our typical portrait of Paul as hierarchical and alienated from women. Perhaps we must rethink our notion of Paul's understanding of the apostolic role as well.

Similarly, in two separate texts Paul speaks of his apostolic role in terms of motherly nurture. In 1 Thessalonians 2:7 Paul says that he and his co-workers "became babes in your midst, as a nurse cherishes her own children" (author's translation). In 1 Corinthians 3:1–2 he laments the spiritual condition of the Corinthian congregation by commenting, "I could not speak to you as spiritual people, but rather as people of the flesh, as infants in Christ. I fed you with milk, not solid food, for you were not ready for solid food." Gaventa speaks of these texts as "metaphors squared," since Paul first images the gospel as maternal milk and then makes the metaphor more complex by placing himself in the role of the mother providing the milk. Unlike metaphors that have to do with paternal "begetting," these maternal metaphors emphasize care that takes place over a period of time.

Something about the task of the apostle, Gaventa claims, makes these images particularly apt.[17] Indeed, Anselm of Canterbury, in the eleventh century, composed a meditation dedicated to Paul that takes these texts as a starting point and addresses Paul as "Sweet nurse, sweet mother,...you are our greatest mother."[18] Ought apostles (and by extension other church leaders, male as well as female) understand their role as engaged in a physical struggle akin to that of childbirth, and a vulnerability that mirrors that involved with caring for a child?[19] If so, Paul is not always so shaped by the strict rules of gender-appropriate behavior and attitudes that we have seen to characterize his social setting.

Making Women Visible

Paul was in many ways a typical man of his day. It seems clear that, except when he turned to deal with "women's issues" (in which women categorically had different concerns than men), he tended to think of his readers as male and address them as such. So, for example, Paul collapses the question of keeping the Law into the question of circumcision, which for his (male) readers represented the keeping of the Law in a very vivid, individual, and personal way. If Paul had been asked, "What about women? Are they free from the Jewish Law, too?" he likely would have said, "Yes, of course; that's just what I've been arguing!" He might even have pointed to his citation of the baptismal formula in Galatians 3:28 to show that what appplied to Jew and Greek applied to male and female as well. But he was not asked, and it did not occur to him.

I hold, then, that the situation of Paul's female readers is less one of exclusion than of invisibility. It is, of course, debatable whether invisibility is preferable to active exclusion, in which the excluded party is recognized as a worthy adversary. Women who experience Paul's letters as projecting active hostility toward them may find a measure of hope in being merely overlooked. At least it opens certain interpretive options. We will explore these options as we continue to consider the letters of Paul.

CHAPTER 2

The World of Paul's Readers

The Myth of Christian Origins

It has become popular in some circles to describe Jesus' behavior toward women as fundamentally radical and absolutely unique, if not in the whole of the world governed by the Roman Empire, then at least in the Palestinian Judaism of which he was a part. It is common to see such claims as "Jesus' new religion was concerned, not about rules, but about people," or "Jesus' behavior would have scandalized the pious Jew."[1] According to this view, in Jesus' time women were expected to be neither seen nor heard outside the home. They did not receive education, and their influence was strictly limited to the upbringing of young children. Strict application of the purity laws kept women secluded for one week every month and caused them to be treated with suspicion whenever they ventured into public. Jesus was the only Jewish male to acknowledge women in public, much less to treat them as human beings and attend to their physical and spiritual needs. The egalitarian community that formed around his ministry was unparalleled in Judaism and was scandalous to other Jews. As the gospel began to be proclaimed outside Palestine, Gentile women, who were, at best, only slightly less oppressed than their Jewish sisters, embraced the movement in all its egalitarianism. The subsequent silencing of women along with the increasing conformity of the church to the social mores of its surroundings is often laid largely at the feet of Paul, whose Jewish conservatism in this regard managed to trump his openness to the teachings of Jesus.

This view is based in part on a misreading, or a superficial reading, of some of the foundational feminist work on Christian origins. Nonetheless it has become a common and pervasive reading, so that those who would counter it find themselves refuting published text after published text. Indeed, the myth morphs to protect its central claims in the face of evidence to the contrary. If women in the Roman Empire are shown to have more freedoms than the model posits, a clear distinction is made between Gentile and Jewish women, then between diaspora and Palestinian Judaism. If women in Jerusalem are shown to be educated, then the distinction is between urban and rural areas. If men and women worship together in synagogues in rural Judea, the line is drawn between Judea and Galilee. The alternative possibility—that the premises themselves are historically inaccurate—seems to be a particularly hard sell.

At times this view has endorsed perspectives that, on the face of them, are strikingly misogynist as well as textually suspect. For example, the portrait, developed over Christian centuries, of Mary Magdalene as a notorious prostitute simply is not supported by the New Testament texts. Yet some contemporary Christian feminists have embraced this view of Mary Magdalene, linking it with references to Jesus' special treatment of her, as evidence for their claim that Jesus had close association with the most marginal and despised female members of society.

To be sure, this story of Christian origins is an attractive one for various reasons. It reinforces the myth of Christian uniqueness by implying that Christianity, alone among all the religions of the world, had gender equality in its founding impetus. It bolsters the position of Christian primitivists (who have existed in various guises, and often with various theological agendas, throughout the church's history) by positing a uniquely nonhierarchical, gender-equal community at the very beginning of Christian existence and by painting every subsequent development as a "fall" from that "state of grace." And it implies that Christians who do not advocate gender equality are somehow untrue to the foundations of their faith—a powerful rhetorical stance.

Like most myths whose reason for existing is primarily theological or apologetic, this one does have important areas of correspondence to the results of historical investigation. It is well established that the world of the first-century Roman Empire was patriarchal and hierarchical in both political and social structures. Women were considered of less value than men, all other social factors being equal. Women's lives were constrained in various ways that did not apply, or did not apply in the same degree, to men. But it is also the case that other factors, particularly social class and economic status, often mattered *more than* gender in determining the responsibilities, freedoms, and constraints that a particular first-century individual experienced. Local factors (such as family, local social structures and economic conditions, or the choices of the local governor or subordinate governmental authority) often mattered more than imperial legislation or decree in determining what laws would be enforced and on whom. Judaism, like other ancient religions, was remarkably varied in theology and practice. While Pharisees may have been vocal in their opinions on the right practice of the law, and strident in their clashes with Jesus, they were a minority in Jewish society. Evidence suggests that non-Pharisees, by and large, did not follow the law with Pharisaic strictness, nor did they particularly worry about incurring the Pharisees' wrath for not having done so. There is no archeological evidence to support the notion that Palestinian Jewish women occupied a separate space within their homes during their monthly period. Indeed, various kinds of ritual impurity were likely quite common, and no one worried much about whether they were pure or impure, unless by chance they were going to the temple that day to worship. Outside Jerusalem, then, the issue of ritual purity would be moot for most people most of the time.[2]

Jesus' openness to women as disciples and his inclusion of them at meals and in his entourage was likely remarkable to many Jews and offensive to some. But this is far from enough to mark him as "unique" or "unparalleled." Rather, he almost certainly fit quite well within what we might today term a "progressive wing" of first-century Judaism. (To be sure, there was a "conservative wing" as well, and perhaps our metaphor should be more on the model of a windmill than an airplane, as Judaism was far too diverse to be split merely into "conservative" and "progressive" camps.) Did detractors identify the women who traveled in Jesus' entourage as "prostitutes"? Almost certainly, but this is not incontrovertible proof that they were, in fact, such. It proves only that the practice of vilifying women's conduct by calling their sexual behavior into question is an ancient as well as modern tactic. Jesus' own behavior toward women, as evidenced in the gospels, seems to have been by turns egalitarian, paternalistic, and downright prejudiced. (See the exchange with the Syrophoenician woman, Mk. 7:25–30.)

In short, then, while some of the history on which it is based is valid, the myth of earliest Christianity as a *uniquely* egalitarian movement is a theologically motivated narrative that supports Christian triumphalism, anti-Judaism, and anti-Catholicism (as the system into which "pure" early

Christianity "fell"). Moreover, it is, according to the best evidence we can accumulate, simply historically wrong. As Kathleen Corley has so aptly put it, "It is a myth of Christian origins, not a historical reconstruction of Christian origins. As a historical reconstruction, it is untenable."[3]

Rethinking Christian Origins

We must, then, revise our understanding of Christianity's earliest origins. It was a relatively progressive movement *within* the variety of first-century Judaism, a movement likely to be particularly attractive to women who had experienced similar freedoms in their previous religious and social experience. With such a revision we not only gain vital historical balance, but we also shift the role of Paul in the relation of women to early Christianity. Paul is no longer the "Judaizer" with regard to the role of women in the Christian community, because no single "Jewish" point of view on women's place either in religion or in society dominated. Nor is Paul, whatever the source of his motivation, rightly seen as the sole or main force quashing the egalitarian impulses of early congregations. Rather, his is one voice in a complicated discussion. As we shall see, Paul does at times advance theological arguments that have the effect of limiting women's expression in worship or in the community. Elsewhere, his remarks lead toward reinforcing the importance and participation of all members of the community, regardless of gender or social status. So it is inappropriate to speak in generalizations, much less to trace Paul's motivation for a particular stance to one facet of his own complicated identity. It is better to lay out the history, such as we can reconstruct it, of the women who were part of Paul's churches, and from there to consider how Paul related to them.

As Bernadette J. Brooten has argued persuasively,[4] study of women in the biblical world has too often focused, not on women themselves and their perspectives, but on men's attitudes toward women, as reflected in men's writings (the literature of the period). Studies of the ancient world that approach this world from the perspective of the classic texts (or, for that matter, the biblical texts) ask the wrong questions. They rely on the wrong sources to obtain the best understanding of the lives, practices, and beliefs of women. Part of the difficulty lies, of course, in the lack of sources. This lack is itself a part of women's history. The lack of a written record points to the lack of importance afforded to women's lives and ideas by those who controlled the means of production of texts.

Brooten adopts Mary Daly's term "prehistory" to emphasize this lack of written history.[5] She stresses that any historical story reconstructed from the available fragments is unavoidably a tentative one. Nonetheless, she insists, the task is not hopeless. Furthermore, the tentative nature of the rendering of women's history from the available fragmentary sources serves to foreground the tentative nature of all historiography. Any historical reconstruction is an "artistic rendering," based not on a foundation of certain and objective knowledge but in the perspectives and biases of the historian, while at the same time it seeks to be based upon and responsible to the available historical evidence.[6]

When women in Paul's congregations are in view, moreover, sociological data that aim at the "average" and the "typical" may fail to represent the particularity of Paul's congregations. Consider the analogy of an imaginary contemporary congregation, formed because its members found themselves at odds with their peers in other congregations or with the general direction of their denomination. A demographic study might look at the larger societal structures to which these individuals belong or seek a general overview of the denomination. In either case the study would miss not only the particular commitments of this congregation but also their very reason for constituting as a congregation in the first place. Wayne Meeks has argued persuasively that a significant number of the leading members of Paul's congregations likely experienced "status inconsistency." This term means they had both low social status markers (such as slave birth or low-status occupation) and high status markers (say, wealth or marriage to a member of a higher social class).[7] These people, then, would be the "atypical" ones for whom large-scale sociological data might fail to account. They would be very significant for the much smaller-scale social structure of a particular Pauline congregation—perhaps one of the very ones to whom Paul wrote a letter that is preserved in our New Testament canon.

Moreover, as Ross Shepard Kraemer points out, the focus on "women's experience" raises a host of thorny methodological issues.[8] Feminist scholars claim to be interested in women's experiences and women's perspectives, as these are unmediated by men. If they must settle for experiences or perspectives mediated by men, they seek to strip away the male viewpoint and reach the viewpoint of the woman or women. This is a valuable quest, made necessary by the often-scant literary production of women and by an androcentric culture's devaluing of those literary products and failure to facilitate their distribution and preservation. However, such a quest risks ignoring the real experiences of those women who experienced satisfaction and fulfillment in what today's feminists identify as oppressive structures of exploitation.

This difficulty highlights the limitations of relying on reported experience, since that experience was perceived according to the dictates of past societal norms and expectations. On the other hand, the very fact we are able to bring to light the ideology that constrained our foremothers makes us uneasily aware that we are ideologically constructed as well. We may seek to uncover the ideological foundations that make certain ideas "natural" and "acceptable" to us while making it impossible to imagine others. Still, we continue to be shaped by factors of which we are unaware. It may well be that a later generation will look back with bemused pity on our inability to recognize our ideological constraints. Perhaps the most daunting task of any generation of feminists is to make peace with our grandmothers. This effort requires us genuinely to respect the perspectives and experiences of those before us (including those whom we study), while identifying the circumstances of their lives as constrained, oppressed, or exploited such that we could never consent to those lives for ourselves.

Our Available Sources

A few comments, then, are in order regarding the nature of our sources. First, we need to recall that most written sources regarding the lives of women in the ancient world were written by males, from a male perspective, and typically from an upper-class perspective as well. Studies of the much-discussed cloistered life of the Roman maiden and matron, for example, emphasize what she is not to do (for example, go out of doors alone, attend public dinners, and so forth). Such study fails to discuss how these women passed their days: frequently in the organization and supervision of a complicated household, including perhaps a fair number of slaves and other retainers, both male and female. Such a discussion also fails to acknowledge that such women represented only the upper stratum of social class in the Roman Empire. In contrast, Christianity apparently drew from a wide variety of social classes. A comparison of "women in early Christianity" with the Roman maidens and matrons, then, gives us a false picture of both groups.

Second, our sources are partial, reflecting both the arbitrariness of chance survival through the centuries and the quite intentional choices of later interpreters to preserve some documents and destroy others. (The latter is the reason, for example, that we have very little documentary evidence from groups later deemed "heretical" by the church.) When few pieces of evidence are available, interpreters sometimes draw sweeping conclusions from very specific data. These conclusions, then, often are repeated without sufficient attention to the narrowness of the data on which they are based. The practice of one local group or congregation is assumed, without further proof, to be the practice of all similar groups or congregations.

Third, we should be cautious in applying modern standards of law to the legal pronouncements of antiquity. True, legal pronouncements of the Roman Empire carried the not-inconsiderable authority of the state. We must recall, however, that local officials had a great deal of license in enforcing the laws. In particular, minority groups might be tolerated or even encouraged in one area while being persecuted in another, all while the imperial government turned a blind eye (unless taxes were going unpaid, or armed rebellion was fomented). Indeed, legal pronouncements, far from leading us to believe that the prohibited action never occurred, should raise the question of whether the action or activity being prohibited was particularly prevalent, so that legal means were being used in an attempt to keep the action or activity within bounds.

Finally, their continued prevalence in New Testament interpretation necessitates a word about the use of rabbinic teachings, primarily the Mishnah and Talmud, as evidence of Jewish perspectives during New Testament times. The Mishnah is a collection of rabbinic teachings with traditions tracing back to the pre-Tannaitic period (from 200 B.C.E.), but the compilation of these traditions, stories, and pronouncements took place centuries later. It is, therefore, highly speculative to use the Mishnah (or other rabbinic texts, most of which postdate the Mishnah in textual form) to demonstrate views held in the New Testament era, particularly prior to the formative crisis that confronted Judaism with the destruction of Jerusalem in 70 C.E.

It is also instructive, particularly for those who have little background in the rabbinic tradition, to reflect on the nature of these texts. Far from being "legal" documents in the sense with which we are generally familiar, these texts reflect debates, disagreements, and differences of opinion among rabbis seen, collectively, as the shapers of the tradition. (Faced with disagreements of similar gravity, Christianity tended to fragment and, frequently, to pronounce anathemas on one another.) Too, the rabbis whose debates are recorded in the Mishnah and other rabbinic texts believed that it was important to determine how the divine law should theoretically be kept, even if their determinations were impossible in practice. For example, the rabbis continued to discuss the proper qualifications for the red heifer for the Day of Atonement sacrifice long after the destruction of the temple, when animal sacrifices ceased. Thus it is difficult to use the rabbinic sources to determine actual practice, even in post-70 C.E. Judaism. Much more so, then, it is nearly impossible to gauge by this thin strand of tradition the wide variety of Jewish faith and practice throughout the Roman world in the first century C.E.

What, then, can we discern about the congregations to whom Paul wrote, and particularly about the women in those congregations? We are concerned primarily with the cities of the eastern part of the Roman Empire, particularly the cities of Asia Minor, Macedonia, and the Attic peninsula, during the first century C.E. Where urban life differed from that of the countryside, we are concerned with the urban. Where life in the city of Rome differed from that of the colonies, we want to know what it was like to live outside Rome itself. The earliest Christian congregations revered the same sacred scriptures as the Jews and were apparently, to varying degrees, associated with the diaspora synagogues and the teachings of Judaism. But Paul's mission was primarily to the Gentiles. Thus while we will attend to Jewish tradition that may have been passed on, we are particularly interested in the Gentile religious background of those who would have been Paul's converts. Finally—and this is the most difficult part—we are primarily concerned with the common rather than the elite class. "Not many [of you] were of noble birth," Paul says to the Corinthians (1 Cor. 1:26), implying that some of them likely were. Still, the majority, and apparently the bulk of Paul's congregations, were made up of people of humble backgrounds. Thus much of our data will of necessity be general, and the crucial step will be our interpretation of it. Nonetheless there are important observations to make about the world in which Paul's first readers and hearers lived. The insights we gain can help us understand how they may have understood his letters.

Women in the First-Century Roman World

Early Hardships

In a society in which basic education is compulsory, basic health care is widely available, and chronic malnutrition is abnormal, it may be difficult to imagine daily life in a situation that lacked what we would think of as the most basic necessities. Yet most readers will not be surprised to discover that, in such a society, women were typically the ones who experienced the greatest hardship from the lack of resources.[9] The stigma of being female began at a girl's birth. Her father, recognizing the financial liability to the family that her upbringing and dowry would bring, had to decide whether she would be kept as a daughter or exposed. Exposure of newborn infants often brought death, of course, but an exposed infant might also be rescued and raised as a slave or, if female, for a trade in which women were needed in large numbers (such as in an inn or a brothel). Some groups, notably Jews and apparently also Christians, seem to have practiced neither exposure of infants nor abortion.[10] Legally, however, the prerogative remained with the father of the child. According to Roman law, only the firstborn daughter had to be raised.[11]

Nor did the risks to a girl's life end if she escaped exposure. Infant mortality was so high in the ancient world that laws prohibited the standard rituals of mourning for children less than one year old. Presumably these deaths were too common to practice the rituals. If the victim were one year up to twelve, a certain portion of the ritual would be enacted. In times of scarcity of food, boys generally received a greater portion than did girls. Thus many girls experienced malnutrition during at least part of their physical development.

Formal education for women was generally seen as unnecessary (although, due to the sweeping nature of paternal prerogative, some girls did receive much more formal education than others). A girl would learn from her mother or other females in the household the tasks essential for running a home. (And depending, of course, on the family's social status and wealth, this could include substantial concerns for household management). If the family were engaged in a trade, she would probably learn to calculate and possibly to read necessary documents of business. More formal education than this, however, was usually reserved for males, as the family's means made possible.

Marriage and Motherhood

Frequent cautions in ancient literature that a woman should pass her first menstruation before she engaged in sexual intercourse provide evidence that girls were married young, barely into puberty. An unmarried daughter was a financial burden and a potential source of embarrassment to her family. Control of her affairs generally transferred, with her marriage, from a young woman's father to her husband. She would be expected to leave the household gods of her childhood and adopt the gods of her husband.[12] Several ancient documents chronicle the fearful prospect of marriage for a young woman, and understandably so, since she often had little preparation for her new tasks, little knowledge of what the future would bring, and little prospect of contact with her family after her marriage.[13]

Thus a woman might become pregnant with her first child while still in her mid-teens, with a body suffering the effects of childhood malnutrition and little or no knowledge of prenatal self-care. Coupled with a very elementary medical understanding of gynecology (medically knowledgeable help was available generally for the upper classes alone), a woman would be dependent on the greatly variable abilities of a midwife to help her through the difficulties of labor and delivery. No wonder childbirth was the greatest threat to the life of a woman who survived her own childhood! No wonder many children were reared by stepmothers, and many a young bride entered a household in which children were already present. Life in the husband's household could involve a supportive, caring network of women in the extended family: a mother-in-law, grandmothers, aunts, daughters, and stepdaughters. On the other hand, these could also be the very people who made a bride's life miserable—and a young woman often had little idea which she would encounter.

Degrees of Seclusion

Roman moral literature of the first century frequently describes an ideal world in which the wife stays at home, out of the public eye. She runs the household so efficiently and competently that the husband, on returning home from a day in public life, has not to lift a finger either in command or direction. He finds everything arranged for his comfort. These same documents, notably, often look back fondly to the "good old days" in which this arrangement held. Such documents opine that "nowadays" women gad about, get involved in all sorts of pursuits without their husbands' permission, and neglect the running of the home. It is difficult to say, of course, whether either the "then" or the "now" is represented in such texts with journalistic accuracy. The general picture that emerges is one of women who have, depending on their social class and the resources at their disposal, a good deal of power. But that power is carefully circumscribed, limited in its exercise, and structured in the service of a society that is unquestioningly androcentric.

It is not unreasonable to guess that a woman's degree of seclusion from the public corresponded, more or less, with her social station. An aristocratic woman would live most of her life out of the public eye, in "women's quarters" of the house, involved in domestic duties and the supervision of domestic servants. Servants and other attendants would accompany her whenever she did venture out. However, her actual influence in society, exercised through her management of the household, might far exceed that of her less affluent sisters. A freewoman of lesser means, or a freedwoman, would necessarily participate in the economic life of the family in ways that required her presence in public, whether selling or buying, serving or negotiating. Lower-class women were engaged in a wide variety of professions: trade (such as grocers and fishmongers), personal services (hairdressers, midwives, tailors, barmaids, and the like), entertainment (dancers, musicians, and so forth), as well as sexual services. Slaves of both genders regularly performed those public tasks that made it possible for their mistresses to remain secluded.

If this is so, we should expect to find in the surviving literature of the period a rather greater emphasis on women's seclusion, as the "ideal" state of affairs, than was actually the case. Too, if our interest is in "common," nonaristocratic women, we may come to realize that it is just these women who were more accustomed to being out in public, to interacting even with men who were not their relatives, and so forth. Presumably, men in the era of the Roman Empire (at least those who bought into the prevailing ideology) would have liked to keep their wives and daughters at home, secluded and surrounded by servants. Apparently few were capable of doing so. How the women would have preferred it, in such a strongly androcentric culture, is difficult to determine.

Too, the situation in society was almost certainly more complicated than the one inscribed in law or imagined in moral literature. True, a woman was almost always legally under the power of some man, whether her father, her husband, or some designee (in the case, for example, of her husband's death). Some women, however, quite capably managed their own affairs, particularly in widowhood, and the guardian remained a legal fiction.[14]

The ideal woman might be one who never appeared in public. For many ordinary people whose livelihood depended on trade, the wife as well as the husband had of necessity to deal with the public to keep the family business going. Given the high rate of childhood mortality, a father might have no sons survive him and so focus his hopes as well as his means on a favored daughter. Even though in some situations the marital situation might be well-nigh unbearable for a wife, some marriages of true mutual love and esteem did exist, characterized not only by lack of conflict but by positive harmony. Paul's readers, then, might have taken the circumscribed social roles of marriage for granted, but looked forward to a happy and fulfilling life within those roles.

Widows and Virgins

The significant presence of widows and virgins in the letters of Paul, both as members of the congregation (e.g., 1 Cor. 7) and as illustrations (e.g., Rom. 7:2–3), is an important clue to the significance of members of these social categories in Paul's churches. The presence in the Pauline tradition of admonitions to keep these women in their proper places (1 Tim. 5:3–16) is further evidence that their role in the congregation was a matter of some dispute. Society strongly connected women's identity with their familial roles. Duties of home and family typically consumed much of a married woman's physical and emotional energy. Unmarried adult women constituted dangerous exceptions to the way ancient society expected individuals to function.

Moreover, a significant number of women spent a part of their adult life as widows. The Romans sought to limit the presence of widows in society, sometimes by legislation requiring prompt remarriage (cf. 1 Timothy's attempt to define "real widows"). Still, it seems clear some widows in the community were destitute and needed assistance. But many widows found that relative freedom from the duties of housekeeping, childbearing, and child rearing left them time and leisure for participating more fully in the life of the church.

Adult virgins, that is, women who had never been married, were likely uncommon in the general population. Again, however, we have reason to suspect that those few women who, for whatever reason, had avoided the near inevitability of marriage might well have gravitated toward a community that seemed to hold singleness in high esteem (1 Cor. 7:8, 25–35).

It is not unrealistic, then, to imagine that Phoebe (Rom. 16:1), Chloe (1 Cor. 1:11), Euodia and Syntyche (Phil. 4:2), or others of the women whom Paul mentions as leaders or co-workers may have been widowed or unmarried. Paul may well have had some of these, or others, in mind when he wrote gender balance into 1 Corinthians 7:32–35. He advises that not only is an unmarried man (such as himself) free to attend to the affairs of the Lord, but also that "the unmarried woman and the virgin are anxious about the affairs of the Lord, so that they may be holy in body and spirit." The social situation, of course, was hardly so equitable. Men retained much greater freedom to remain "unencumbered" than did women. Even a virgin or widow would be under the legal authority of some man, whether a father, son, or some other male relative. To claim that the situation was unusual in the larger society, though, is to miss the narrower point: Paul's congregations did include women without husbands, and these women, as society's "abnormalities," likely often functioned in ways that were counter to societal norms.

The Religious Life of Women

It is difficult to speak of religious practice in the first-century Roman world without making generalizations so sweeping that they nearly cease to be worthwhile. If first-century Judaism was, as we have already posited, remarkably varied in theology and practice, at least it was unified by reverence for one God, a set (although still somewhat fluid) of sacred texts, and more or less a common history. What Christian interpreters have often lumped together as "pagan" religion, however, represented many deities, often in complex relationships with one another; diverse historical and cultural backgrounds; and widely varied expectations of adherents. Add distinctions of class and gender to the mix, and the result is a complex and sometimes confusing variety of religious expression.

By Paul's time the Roman Empire was geographically vast, ranging from the Atlantic Ocean to the Euphrates River, encompassing northern Africa and most of modern Europe. Much of this region, particularly in the East, had been taken over from the empire of Alexander the Great. Greek influence (known as *Hellenism*) was still strong. Indeed, a traveler in the eastern Roman Empire could get along with Greek alone, although Latin was the *lingua franca* further west. Lower classes, by and large, retained their native tongues (Aramaic in the province of Judea, for example). Similarly, local deities and worship practices often persisted, sometimes superficially Hellenized or Romanized. In addition, the worship of Greek or Roman divine beings was typically introduced, and deities from one area might begin to be revered in another (devotion to Egyptian goddesses and gods was particularly popular throughout the empire). A traveling Christian evangelist, then, was likely to encounter a significant variety of deities and worship practices in various parts of the Roman world.

Polytheism

Foundational to understanding religion in the first-century Roman world is the concept of polytheism. Various aspects of human life were attributed to one divine being or another. Religious practice, in the sense of acknowledgement of the appropriate deity, was woven into every facet of both public and private life, from guarding a city's welfare to performing the most menial of daily tasks. On the other hand, many of the primary deities, particularly of the Roman pantheon, were seen as being indifferent to the situation of ordinary individuals. To seek personal protection or relief, persons sought out still other deities or engaged in various magical practices. Perhaps the most important point to note is that polytheism is, by its nature, *accumulative*. Showing honor to more gods might increase the likelihood of one's own well-being, as well as of protecting one's family, clan, or region. Thus new deities and new rites were generally welcomed by Roman governmental authorities. (An exception might be made if the rites were deemed injurious to public order; but even so, there seems to have been a general stance of wide latitude.) Nor was it difficult to add new divine beings to the pantheon—either the local deities of cultures absorbed by the Roman Empire, or the emperors, to whom increasing devotion was encouraged through the course of the first century.[15]

The notion that a deity might require exclusive devotion of his or her adherents was unknown among most of the cultures that made up the Roman Empire. Monotheism, such as Jews and Christians practiced, often appeared to their neighbors as a form of atheism. They saw it as not only risky to its adherents but also likely to threaten the stability and welfare of the city or the Empire. (Jews, however, were tolerated for the most part on account of the antiquity of their religion, which tended to be held in high esteem by Roman authorities for that reason. Gentile Christians received no such benefit of the doubt and so were often seen as suspect.) Moreover, not only did different deities have different "responsibilities," so to speak, but they interacted with humans in different ways. Thus religious life involved a variety of practices, carried out in different times and places, with varying levels of female participation.

Public Worship

Every city in the Roman Empire had at least one patron deity, whose role was understood as ensuring the welfare of the city and protecting it in times of conflict. These gods or goddesses would be honored with temples in the city, including an altar for animal sacrifice (usually carried out by professionals, typically male). Regular civil festivals involved feasting, processions, and games or contests. All residents of the city would be expected to take part in these celebrations, although roles in the "production" of the festival were markers of prestige and might vary according to gender and social station. Nonetheless, in the Greco-Roman world religious offices were routinely bestowed on those who could afford to sponsor the requisite festivals and sacrifices. While more men than women fit these criteria, women of means willing to be benefactors seem to have encountered little resistance.

Women did serve as religious functionaries in some Greco-Roman temples in menial or sexual tasks. But it remains inappropriate to categorize women's public roles in religious practice as mainly or even largely cultic prostitution. The roles women filled in public religious life in the Roman Empire reflected those of women in society at large. Women occupied a wide variety of positions ranging from forced service and outright exploitation to positions of considerable respect, honor, and influence.

It makes sense to argue that with the evangelization of the Gentiles (in which Paul, he proudly claims, held a pivotal role) came a shift in Christian expectations of the place of women in cultic offices. We must be careful, at this juncture, not to imply that Judaism was misogynistic in a way the pagan religions were not. As we have noted, this presumption, which seeks to make Jesus and the community around him more distinctive by depicting the surrounding society as exceptionally oppressive, stems from a selective reading of the available evidence. Recent scholarship has increasingly unmasked such readings as biased and inaccurate.[16]

Jews shared with their Gentile neighbors a worldview that placed females unquestionably beneath males in the hierarchy of values. Nonetheless, as Bernadette Brooten has demonstrated, some wealthy women apparently did hold honorary offices and function in roles of leadership and influence in Greco-Roman synagogues.[17] Still, during the period with which we are concerned, Jewish women apparently did not generally hold the title "priest."

We do not have conclusive evidence that they performed priestly functions, whereas pagan women in various cults both held such titles and performed such functions.[18] Thus a Jewish woman might come to believe in Jesus as the Christ and join a community of such believers. When she did, she would be unlikely to assume, based on her prior religious experience, that she might become a religious functionary in that community (whether or not, as life in the community went on, she might happen to do so). A female pagan convert to Christianity could be quite likely, based on *her* prior religious experience, to assume that she might acquire a leadership role (again, whether or not this experience was actually borne out in the life of the community).

Private Worship and Devotion

While public civil rites and festivals held an important place in the religious life of residents of the first-century Roman Empire, many people engaged in other forms of religious expression as well. Individuals often belonged to certain groups by virtue of their social class, job, or economic function; home town; or some other societal marker. They might join a group by choice, based on interests in common with other members. These voluntary associations, each identified by devotion to a particular deity, were less "public" than the civil rites, but they were not secret enclaves. Members were generally expected to pay dues, attend meetings at which particular activities took place, and carry out certain responsibilities as necessary. The activities and responsibilities varied, of course, depending on the nature of the group. Common practices included celebratory feasts on ritual occasions and participation in deceased members' funeral and burial rites. (Such functions were particularly important in groups whose members were poorer and likely could not have afforded a burial without the assistance of the community.) Membership, naturally, depended on the nature of the common thread connecting the group, but women often participated alongside men and sometimes functioned as sponsors or leaders.

Yet another avenue of religious expression was found in secret societies or mystery religions, so called because members were initiated in a secret rite understood to communicate some sort of esoteric knowledge or "mystery" to members only. Mystery religions offered their members eternal life by promising permanent relationship of the initiate with the deity. Not surprisingly, these forms of religious expression often displayed the most intense devotion both to the divinity and to the community. We must reemphasize, however, that practice of a mystery religion did not imply any sort of monotheistic faith on the part of adherents. Rather, for many people the practice of the mystery religion met the need for an experience of close connection or communion with the divine, a dimension often lacking in civic or societal rites. Others sought a similar sense of communion or control in various practices of magic. The practice of a mystery religion could be an expensive undertaking. The initiate usually bore the cost of initiation (often involving animal sacrifice and various, often complicated, other rituals), but it appears that these groups were typically egalitarian about who could be admitted to their ranks—assuming ability to pay.

Gender-Segregated Communities

While many forms of first-century religious expression took place in gender-integrated communities, gender-segregated practices also had an important role. Since classical Greek times, women's religious rites apparently focused largely on women's transitions from one societally acceptable role to another—maiden (presexual) to mother (sexual), mother to crone (postsexual). While these rites, then, reinforced an ideology that identified women with their sexual roles and clarified "good" and "bad" roles, they also encouraged women to value themselves within these roles. Moreover, the rites themselves involved the overturning of the acceptable—proper maidens playing the part of wild animals, the sharing between women of bawdy jokes and raucous laughter at men's expense. Such activities both reinforced the "normal" expectations of the social order and, inevitably, revealed that these expectations were constructed ones. Some of these rituals were secret, while others had practices that were generally known. Not all the religious rites primarily celebrated by women were life-transition ceremonies. Some, apparently, were regularly observed events during which women for a short time left behind the responsibilities of home and family and celebrated in the company of other women. Such respites may have served to reinforce social structures by providing a safe outlet for frustrations, but they also reinforced in women a self-understanding as religious participants.

Many divine figures transcended their original locale to gain acceptance more widely in the Greco-Roman world. Women particularly embraced several of these. For example, Kraemer demonstrates the complicated dynamic of the worship of Isis (who, she says, is identified by many scholars as the main contender with Christianity in the Roman Empire).[19] The myth is long and somewhat complicated: Widowed when her brother-husband Osiris is thrown into the Nile by another brother, Typhon, Isis wanders the world until she locates Osiris's body. Along the way, Isis also discovers that Osiris had fathered a child by another sister, and she adopts this son, Anubis. After Isis finds and mourns over Osiris's body, Typhon steals it yet again, dismembers it, and distributes the pieces all over Egypt. Isis, still faithful to her dead husband, continues to search until she reassembles all the pieces (only the phallus remains missing, and a substitute must be fashioned). She reanimates Osiris long enough for him to impregnate her with another child—who is, unfortunately, born in untimely fashion and with weak legs. Thus Isis's story summarizes the experiences and socially expected roles of many women: sisterhood, marriage, and widowhood; care for children, the sick, and the dead; love, betrayal, and bereavement; loyalty and unswerving devotion.[20]

The story of Isis offered women a powerful goddess with whom to identify, as well as a woman who experienced a full range of human emotions. But Isis's story also reinforces an androcentric ethic: she puts her husband and her son before herself, subordinates herself to them, and tolerates her husband's adultery while keeping herself chaste. Both women and men became devotees of Isis, quite possibly because both were eager to find the marital bliss of which Isis was seen as protectoress. Isis was also seen, in part because her story entailed such suffering, as a divine intercessor on behalf of human sufferers. Worship of Isis, then, while not overturning old societal roles, reshaped them toward somewhat greater individuality and emphasis on the nuclear rather than the extended family. Most importantly, it focused on a strong, active goddess not constrained within the Roman pantheon. As Kraemer says, "[a]t least at the explicit level, the religion of Isis was more favorable to women than any other religion."[21]

For many women, the primary locus of religious activity would have been the home. There the wife/mistress of the house would have played a significant role. Deities honored by one's own family or clan often received obesiance in ceremonies based in the home. These ceremonies involved the dedication of food, drink, or household objects. The proper functioning of the household, indeed, was assumed to require the participation of (or at least lack of interference from) the divine realm. Since the food and objects involved were typically under a woman's purview, she normally would have performed these religious rites as well, either on the family's behalf or in their presence. Women, too, were often primary in the ritually important act of preparing the dead for burial. Given that their domestic practices often carried religious significance, it is easy to imagine how women would have assumed a role of religious leadership in the early Christian communities as well, as those groups gathered in private homes. The religious nature of such acts as the preparation and serving of meals, and the role in the community conferred by the execution of such acts, could easily become a matter of theological discussion and debate.

Named Women in Paul's Congregations

It is not surprising that the earliest Christians, who met in the homes of members whose houses had space to host them, would count women among the leaders of these house congregations. However, women's functions were apparently *not* limited to providing the space to meet and the food for the common meal. Paul takes it for granted that these women are influential in their congregations. Because he takes their leadership for granted, many interpreters overlook their significance.[22]

Euodia and Syntyche

In Philippians 4:2, in the midst of a series of exhortations to unity, Paul urges Euodia and Syntyche to "be of the same mind in the Lord" and goes on to ask his "loyal companion" (presumably another of the church's leaders) to assist in their reconciliation. Their reconciliation is important, says Paul, because they have "struggled beside me in the work of the gospel," that is, they have served as Paul's co-workers in the task of proclamation. Not only were these women important to Paul's work, but they were clearly significant in the Philippian congregation as well. They were important enough that a disagreement between them, whatever the subject (and we are not told why they are not "of the same mind"), threatens the fellowship of the Philippian congregation as a whole.[23] Should it not be immediately obvious to contemporary interpreters that Paul both acknowledges and welcomes the leadership of women in his churches? Yet his very matter-of-fact way of speaking of these women fails to gain the attention of many readers. Thus we go on assuming that Paul did not approve of women's leadership in his churches.

Nympha

Similarly, in Colossians (a text of disputed authorship—see chapter 6), greetings are sent to Nympha and the church in her house (Col. 4:15), acknowledging without comment both a woman's apparent role as head of household and her role as leader of the congregation.[24]

Apphia

Another interesting, and even more overlooked, reference occurs at Philemon 1–2, where Paul addresses his letter specifically to three people: Philemon "the beloved, and our co-worker" (author's translation), Archippus "our fellow soldier," and, between these two, "Apphia our sister."[25] One of these men, presumably Philemon, is being called on by Paul to make a determination regarding his slave, Onesimus, who is returning to him with this letter from Paul. But what of Apphia? Why is she named in the salutation?

In his *Anchor Bible* commentary on Philemon, Joseph Fitzmyer states that Apphia is "a Christian woman who is otherwise unknown," but since she is called *adelphe*, he deduces that she is "a Christian 'sister' to Paul" and likely Philemon's wife or sister, or possibly the wife of Archippus.[26] "In any case," Fitzmyer comments, "as the lady of the house, she would have had to deal constantly with the household slaves." Not a possibility, according to Fitzmyer, is that Apphia is "also a church leader," since he notes that "such a meaning of *adelphe* is nowhere attested."[27]

I would argue, though, that Fitzmyer, like many commentators before him, has missed the point of Apphia's presence in the salutation. He works with assumptions that are nowhere supported in the text while overlooking less speculative possibilities. Apphia may, indeed, be related by marriage or by blood to either Philemon or Archippus (although if she is Archippus's wife the listing of her name before his would be worthy of investigation), but her familial or marital relationship is not what is of primary importance to Paul. Nor is there any indication that Onesimus was specifically a house-servant, such that her involvement as "lady of the house" would be necessary in determining Onesimus's disposition. Rather, Paul addresses her as "our sister," a title that strongly suggests (from Paul's frequent usage of the plural *adelphoi*, "brothers [and sisters]") that she is being addressed as a member of the Christian community. Her leadership within that community, then, would be logically deduced from two facts. She is named along with one or two male leaders of the community (depending on whether the slaveowner is also a church leader), and the rest of the church is mentioned without singling out individuals, "the church in your house." As Fitzmyer correctly notes, Philemon is not a private letter, but addressed specifically to the believing community: "Paul is concerned that the whole community that gathers in prayer at Philemon's house be involved in the way Onesimus is to be welcomed back by Philemon."[28]

Apphia's inclusion in the salutation, then, indicates that she is a person of influence in that community, or, to put it briefly, a leader of the church. Arguments otherwise perpetuate the mistaken assumption that Paul did not acknowledge or commend the leadership of women in his churches. Moreover, by being thus named she is called as a witness, and apparently the chief witness, to Paul's directive to Philemon. Clearly, here is a woman who has a place of both influence and authority. Significantly, she is called upon as a witness precisely at the occasion when the church is expected to confront, as one feminist commentator describes it, "a 'test case' of liberating praxis."[29] Apphia is prominent among those who will judge Paul's letter, Philemon's response, and the congregation's ability to revision the way God works among them to shape a community out of both slave and free.

Phoebe

Perhaps the best example of Paul's commendation of women for tasks of leadership in the church comes in the greetings of Romans 16. The chapter begins with a commendation for Phoebe, who is described as a "deacon" (*diakonos*) of the church at Cenchreae. Since Paul asks the letter's recipients to welcome and assist her, presumably she is a traveler, carrying Paul's letter to the congregation at Rome.[30] This fact would suggest that Phoebe is a businesswoman, and likely a person of some means. The impression is reinforced, furthermore, by Paul's comment that she has been a "benefactor of many and of myself as well" (Rom. 16:2). The Greek word *prostatis*, "benefactor," suggests one who administers charitable activities out of personal wealth; although the feminine form of the noun appears here, the masculine form of the same noun (*prostates*) becomes a technical term in Jewish literature. Thus Phoebe, a well-to-do woman, is apparently not only a financial supporter of the gospel mission but also a participant, both in her own congregation in an official capacity, and in her role as the trusted envoy of Paul to Rome.

Other Women in Romans 16

Nor is Phoebe the only woman named in this chapter. Of the twenty-six persons named in verses 3–15, nine are women. More women than men get special mention by Paul for their church activity. Prisca, along with her husband Aquila, is named as Paul's co-worker who has risked her life for Paul and who hosts a house church (v. 4). It is unusual to see the woman's name listed first. This practice implies that Prisca is the more prominent member of the couple, possibly because she is of higher social class but perhaps more likely because she is the more important church leader.

Mary (v. 6) is commended for having "worked very hard among you." Junia is listed with her husband Andronicus. Notably, both members of the couple are identified as "apostles," a title which Paul defends vigorously when he applies it to himself. "Apostle," for Paul, clearly means a certain kind of religious authority, so it is significant here that he applies it to a woman.[31] Paul holds this couple in particularly high regard, not only because they had been imprisoned for the gospel along with him but also because they were believers even before Paul. (Here, incidentally, we get a very brief glimpse of the earliest church before Paul's mission.)

Tryphaena and Tryphosa are "workers in the Lord," and Persis has "worked hard in the Lord" and is given the title "the beloved" (v. 12). The mother of Rufus is not named, but Paul commends her as "a mother to me also" (v. 13). Finally, a list of greetings without further designation includes Julia and the sister of Nereus (v. 15).

This list is notable because so many women appear in it and because Paul commends them for their work. The list is also remarkable for the casual, almost offhand way Paul lists these women who work in the ministry of the church. It appears that their participation in the proclamation of the gospel is nothing unusual.

Imagining the Larger Picture

This list opens a small window onto what we must imagine was a much larger reality. Women, a remarkable number of women given the physical and social constraints of the time, were active in the ministry of the gospel—individually, in couples, and as members of extended families. They proclaimed (and were imprisoned for their proclamation), hosted churches, served in official capacities, assisted financially, and did all manner of work required to keep the Christian community functioning. Paul knows of their work and commends it. Apparently he is personally close to some of these women as well. All of this is evidence for a different way of reading Paul. We may legitimately, these texts suggest, think of Paul as one who knows and supports women's ministry. We may read him with a bias in favor of women in mind. What he has to say on particular occasions about particular situations, then, is our topic for further investigation.

CHAPTER 3

Paul and His Churches

In the Corinthian correspondence we get our best perspective on Paul's ongoing relationship with a congregation, in all its twists, turns, and complications. Paul apparently founded the Corinthian congregation and retained a close relationship with it. Still, the congregation retained the autonomy to consider the preaching of traveling evangelists other than Paul. They also reserved their right to listen to theological and ethical reflection of members of their own congregation, including, apparently, some of the women of the congregation. We do not know exactly what Paul preached when he founded this congregation, of course. We do not even have his first written communication with them (1 Cor. 5:9 mentions a previous letter). Neither do we have any of the Corinthians' letters to Paul (1 Cor. 7:1 says he is discussing "matters about which you wrote"). Other communications from Paul to the Corinthians may have been lost as well. Nonetheless, the extant correspondence is sufficient for us to develop a rather detailed picture of Paul's relationship with this congregation, as he constructs it rhetorically, and to gain insight into the issues in the Corinthian church of particular interest to women.

The Corinthian Church: Social Status and Social Roles

As has been previously suggested, Gentile women entering the Christian community were somewhat more likely than their Jewish sisters to assume that they might hold positions of leadership, based on their previous religious experience. Particularly since the Corinthian congregations[1] met in homes and shared meals together, the relatively upper-class women who hosted the gatherings and oversaw the preparation of food might be expected to be influential members of the community. Paul's reference in 1 Corinthians to "Chloe's people" (1:11) as the ones who have communicated to him news about the congregation probably points to one of these women. In all likelihood Chloe was a widow managing the estate left by her late husband, handling business dealings, and working with slaves and clients who might well be referred to collectively as "her people." In addition to purely business relationships, however, at least some of this retinue apparently also participated with Chloe in the church of which she was a member. Thus their travel on business on her behalf could easily be combined with visits to their founder and mentor Paul, perhaps to see to his welfare, and certainly to bring him news of the congregation and seek his counsel.

But was Chloe the only woman at Corinth with this kind of power and influence? "Not many [of you] were of noble birth," says Paul (1:26). Still, many of the problems he describes in the Corinthian church give evidence of class divisions, and the text is rhetorically freighted with Paul's assertion of his own authority. Were the divisions in Corinth based in gender as well as social class? Following the work of Antoinette Clark Wire,[2] feminist scholars have frequently pointed to Paul's rather tense and rhetorically charged discussions of women's roles in the church in 1 Corinthians to argue that Paul's authority was, in fact, challenged by a group of charismatically gifted women in Corinth. They disagreed with Paul on some important points of theology and church polity. These women might well have become influential in the church because the congregation met in their homes. As Gentile women they would have been accustomed to assuming an important role in religious practice. They may have assumed leadership because they prepared and served the fellowship meal that was such a significant part of the community's gatherings (cf. 1 Cor. 11:20–22). Moreover, Gentile religious practices that had to do with receiving inspired messages or oracles from the gods frequently recognized priestesses as the vehicles of those messages. In the charismatic community at Corinth, women may have seen themselves as taking on a similar role. In any case, it is clear that issues of gender were part of the tension within the congregation at Corinth, and that Paul had to negotiate these issues in his correspondence with them.

Marriage and Singleness "In View of the Coming Age"

Paul first addresses gender issues directly in 1 Corinthians 7. He begins with the pithy comment: "It is well for a man not to touch a woman" (7:1). This epigram, in earlier interpretation often attributed to Paul himself, is now widely recognized as a quotation from the Corinthian congregation's correspondence to him (and is punctuated as such in most modern translations).[3] Paul goes on both to agree and to take issue with the statement. He affirms also the appropriateness of marriage and marital relations, but qualifies what he says with the reasoning "because of cases of sexual immorality" (7:2), hardly a ringing endorsement for the positive value of marriage. Moreover, Paul states that his advice to marry is "of concession, not of command" (7:6) and indicates his preference for his own practice of celibacy. Yet, what Paul does say to commend marital relations in this text is strikingly evenhanded, stating that both the husband and the wife "have authority" (*exousiazo*) over one another's bodies. The precise nuance of Paul's attitude toward marriage in this text has been a subject of debate throughout the history of the church. It is nonetheless clear that he recognizes certain differences in practice as being acceptable and that he specifically includes women along with men as responsible agents in matters of sexuality.

The rest of chapter 7 is counsel to various members of the church, based on their age and marital status—young or old; single, married, divorced, widowed, or about to be married. Again, the text is remarkable in the predominance of an evenhanded tone as regards gender. Through most of the chapter, Paul instructs his readers as if women had the same freedom to choose their sexual and marital status as men. In general, the advice is to maintain the status quo whenever possible. Those who are single or widowed should remain single; those who are married should not seek divorce. Even those who are engaged are commended for not going through with the marriage—unless, of course, the more serious problem of uncontrollable desire recommends marriage as the better option.

Paul's Rule and Roman Practice

Paul states his "rule" three times in verses 17–24, expanding it to cover matters other than marital status. Whether one is married or single, circumcised or uncircumcised, slave or free, "let each of you remain in the condition in which you were called" (7:20).[4] Several verses later, we learn the rationale behind this profoundly conservative social advice. Paul believes that "the appointed time has grown short" (7:29) and the crisis accompanying the end of the world is imminent. In view of such considerations, then, he counsels focus on the work of the Lord rather than distraction by practices that change one's social status.

Paul's advice in 1 Corinthians 7, which has been taken both as a recommendation of celibacy and an encouragement of marriage, was by no means a culturally "safe" set of prescriptions. As Margaret MacDonald has demonstrated, the early Christian communities were not the first to practice celibacy. The ancient Greek philosophical tradition, in particular, recognized the value of celibacy to a philosophical life.[5] But to commend celibacy in itself, and not just to those who had a particular philosophical predilection, would almost certainly have risked Paul running afoul of the Roman authorities.

It is, of course, exceedingly difficult to legislate marital and sexual practices. It is even more difficult to determine, from a historical perspective, the situations that gave rise to particular laws and how those laws were respected and enforced throughout the Roman Empire. Still, we know that the Roman authorities in the first century sought to make marriage obligatory between the ages of twenty and fifty.[6] They sought to require remarriage after divorce or widowhood. They also put into place a system of rewards and punishments by which women who did not produce children experienced limitations, such as restrictions on inheritance, and women who had produced several children received privileges, such as the ability to conduct their legal affairs without a guardian.[7] In such a context the commendation of the single life, particularly for women, and the encouragement for widows not to remarry would have been viewed askance if it were thought to be influential enough to make a difference in the larger society.

Female and Male: Different Experiences

The difference between singleness/celibacy and marriage/sexuality was experienced differently by women and men.[8] The issue was rarely one of autonomy. A woman was, legally, under her father's control before she married and (in most cases) under her husband's control afterward, although the way a particular father or husband chose to exercise that control could vary.[9] The sexual relations that accompanied marriage, though, often led to pregnancy and childbirth, the most serious risks to a young woman's life and health in the ancient world. Thus quite reasonably many women feared such relations. A woman who managed to bring a child into the world would have to acquiesce to her husband's decisions concerning it, and infant mortality was strikingly common. Besides these dangers and potential grief, a woman leaving her parents' home for marriage might have to face the reality of breaking all her previous emotional ties. She might never see family and childhood friends again, while men who married remained connected to their families (often becoming responsible, eventually, for aged relatives). Small wonder that women, specifically, found the possibility of singleness and freedom from sexuality in the context of a community that would protect them against destitution particularly attractive.[10]

Female Freedom

What is yet more remarkable, and often overlooked, about 1 Corinthians 7 is the degree of freedom Paul offers women, in particular, to make decisions regarding their own marital/sexual status. No doubt Paul's own predilection for celibacy was a contributing factor. He valued the celibate life for himself and for other believers, understanding it to help the believer focus on the things of God without worldly distraction. Very likely Paul knew celibate Christian women, who may have made up some of the co-workers he mentions in his letters. He had opportunity to observe and respect their way of life. Modern readers may not grasp the full significance, though, of Paul's explicitly extending this decision to women as well as men in the believing community. Although, admittedly, men sometimes seem to be directed to make decisions on women's behalf (1 Cor. 7:27, 36–38), the pattern in the chapter is strikingly reciprocal.

Females were commonly understood to be less spiritual and more carnal than males, so that a woman could transcend her base nature only by renouncing her sexuality and "becoming male." In such a society it would have been logical for Paul to speak to male believers about controlling women's sexuality (along the lines of what we see in 1 Cor. 7:36–38) and simply to encourage women toward the celibate life. Such a course of action would go along with the common understanding that women were too easily swayed by their emotions to be trusted with such significant decisions. Yet Paul does not follow this line of reasoning. Rather, he presumes that female believers in his Corinthian congregation have nearly the same responsibilities to make decisions about their marital and sexual status as the male believers do. He advises widows as if they have full choice in deciding whether to remarry (7:39–40). If, indeed, the Corinthian congregation extended this measure of autonomy to women in the area of marriage, this would be a strikingly egalitarian practice in the larger society of which it was a part.

Paul and Divorce

Within this discussion of marriage and sexuality, 1 Corinthians 7:10–16 is curious in many ways, not the least of which is the way Paul apparently first cites, then modifies, a "word of the Lord." Paul rarely claims a "word of the Lord" for his teaching, although he frequently makes it clear that his apostolic status stands behind what he says. Here, though, he cites the "word of the Lord" against divorce. Whether this is to be understood as a Jesus tradition or that of the risen Christ present in the community is unclear. Paul's words do bear strong resemblance to the Synoptic tradition of Jesus' prohibition of divorce (Mk. 10:2–12 pars). Nonetheless, no sooner has Paul cited this "word" than he modifies it to provide contingencies should divorce take place. He then goes on to give his own word, specifically *not* that of "the Lord," that a believing spouse should not leave an unbelieving spouse, for the possible salvation of the unbelieving spouse and the "holiness" of the children. If an unbelieving spouse demands the separation, however, the believing spouse should acquiesce. All of these regulations, interestingly, are made reciprocal, with either the husband or wife (whichever is the believing spouse receiving Paul's teaching) made responsible for the decision.

What is going on here? Why does Paul give, then modify, a "word of the Lord"? Apparently Paul's theological and moral principles are clashing with his pastoral concerns. This tells us, in turn, something about the events happening in the Corinthian congregation. Paul knows that divorce is against a "word of the Lord," but he is also aware that divorce is taking place in the congregation. He does not think that all these divorces are theologically equal. So he nuances the rule: Christians should not initiate divorce; this is clearly against the "word of the Lord." Nor should they give up on a previous marital relationship. They should seek reconciliation, and they should not remarry. (This last precept, incidentally, flies in the face of Augustan—and later—proclamations that divorcées, like widows, under fifty years of age should remarry within a relatively short period of time.) But a believer whose spouse has insisted on divorce should not refuse. "In such a case," says Paul, "the brother or sister is not bound" (1 Cor. 7:15). Presumably believers' nonbelieving spouses, wives as well as husbands, were seeking divorce from the believers, and Paul concurs with these separations on the grounds of "peace."

It is fascinating to wonder, though, if yet more is involved here. We know almost nothing of Paul's personal background from his letters, except that he is a proud Jew of diaspora heritage and that he "was…zealous for the traditions of [his] ancestors" (Gal. 1:14), apparently at a young age before his experience of the risen Christ. Acts gives us very little more to go on. We need to be careful not to read too much from later rabbinic tradition back into Paul's life. The articulation of the requirement that all rabbis must be married, for example, postdates Paul by as much as two hundred years. Still, one is curious whether Paul's apparently deep pastoral concern for believers abandoned by their spouses draws from a yet deeper spring.

Could there stand behind it the untold story of a young woman from a respectable diaspora Jewish family, married or promised in marriage to the promising young rabbi from Tarsus? Is it possible that she could not abide the disgrace that his change of heart brought on the family and so returned to her father's house? Might this be accompanied by the story of a Paul who, grieving, let her go? We have, of course, no way of knowing. The tenderness of Paul's pastoral concern for the abandoned spouse (even the abandoned husband, who theoretically could have had the legal power to compel his wife to stay with him) suggests personal knowledge of the painful consequences of insistence on the divorce prohibition.

Conclusions from 1 Corinthians 7

In sum, Paul seems generally to prefer singleness and celibacy, particularly for those who intend to carry out the work of the Lord. He often speaks as if the marital relationship is little more than a concession to weakness (7:9, 28, 37–38) or even a positive hindrance to one's divine calling (7:32–35). He makes it clear that voluntary singleness is his personal choice. As elsewhere in his letters, he is not hesitant to recommend himself, directly or indirectly, as a model for imitation. Yet as we have already noted, Paul treats women's leadership in his congregations as an unremarkable phenomenon. Additionally, he seems to refer to more couples as church leaders than any other New Testament writer (Prisca and Aquila, Rom. 16:3; Andronicus and Junia, Rom. 16:7; Philemon and Apphia—or possibly Apphia and Archippus—Philem. 1–2). Granted, we know little about these pairs, and it is possible that they may have been siblings or celibate ministry teams. Likeliest, though, is that they were married couples, sharing responsibilities for proclamation, ministry, and congregational leadership. Perhaps Paul was too focused on his own practices of ministry to recognize the strengths these couples exhibited and to commend them to his readers. It is clear, however, that Paul did not, in his ministry or in the congregations in which he had influence, limit leadership either to males or to the celibate.

1 Corinthians 11:2–16 and 14:33b–36:
Veiled, Silent, or What?!

First Corinthians 14:34 commands that "women should be silent in the churches." This is likely the text most frequently quoted to demonstrate Paul's misogyny and opposition to women's religious leadership. The text comes from a letter widely agreed to be authentically Pauline.[11] The command seems to be a blanket one backed up by both the witness of "the Law" and the practice of "all the churches." What options are open for the interpretation of this challenging text?

First, it is important to take stock of the wider context of the text, and particularly of a companion text a few chapters earlier in the same letter, 1 Corinthians 11:2–16. Although this text has some difficulties of its own, as we will see below, the entire argument is clearly grounded on the presupposition that women will pray and prophesy in the assembly—the very thing the 1 Corinthians 14 passage seems to prohibit. In short, then, it is not possible to take both 1 Corinthians 11 and 1 Corinthians 14 at face value, unless one concludes that Paul is simply too self-contradictory to be a reliable guide for church practice. Let us, then, turn to each of these passages, examine what is happening in it, and consider the interpretive options.

1 Corinthians 11:2–16

First Corinthians 11:2–16 begins with a call for imitation and a commendation to the Corinthians for carrying on in "the traditions" (*tas paradoseis*, "that which is handed on"). The exhortation and commendation together represent a strong rhetorical signal that Paul is about to venture into controversial territory in which he wants his readers to acknowledge his authority. Thus, we will not be surprised if we discover that the arguments that follow do not support his claim directly. The arguments seem rather to be persuasive only to the already persuaded—that is, those who recognized Paul's authority already, as he intended for them to do. Such persuaded readers would find comfort in evidence that bolstered their impression that Paul was, indeed, right.

The problem Paul finally identifies in verse 5 is apparently that of women praying and prophesying in the assembly with uncovered heads. (The counterexample in verse 4 of men who pray and prophesy with covered heads does not seem to be part of the real issue, since the thread does not reappear in Paul's argument.) Paul's visceral revulsion to such behavior was culturally grounded. Respectable women in Paul's day wore their hair up and covered. Presumably some of the Corinthian women had removed their head covering and let their hair flow down freely to express their Christian freedom. Such a woman would have been widely understood as lewd, advertising the availability of her sexual services.

Paul apparently assumes that the Corinthian women are not, in fact, engaged in sexual immorality, as Paul defines that morality elsewhere. Still, he likely saw the Corinthian women's behavior as not only inappropriate but positively dangerous, both for the community and the women themselves. Women's bodies were, as Dale Martin has perceptively demonstrated, seen as more "porous," more susceptible to defilement than men's bodies. Women were viewed as inherently more sexually charged than men. Since a connection was held to exist between the genitals and the head, the veil functioned in two important ways. The veil protected a woman from the outside world, including supernatural forces that might invade her body during the vulnerable moment of the reception of prophecy. It also protected others (namely, males) from her dangerous sexuality.[12]

That Paul does not recognize his own logic as being either culturally or medically grounded, however, is clear in the arguments he advances for his position. In themselves, the proofs are weak, and even Paul admits the flaws of one of them.

Paul's first argument for the veiling of women who pray or prophesy is based on the word *kephale*, "head." The key issue for Paul's argument is the woman's "head." The Greek *kephale* means "head" in the sense both of "authority" and "source." Paul's argument is a hierarchical one: Christ is to man as husband is to wife as God is to Christ.[13] If this hierarchy holds, then it would ground the practice of insisting on women's head-covering and men's bareheadedness in a theological, rather than simply traditional, justification. Paul sees the logic of his argument in both senses of the word *kephale*: Woman is made both "from" (*ek*) man (v. 8, source) and "for" (*dia*) man (v. 9, authority). Yet Paul has hardly made his point before he sees it start to unravel. Human experience, even in Paul's day, was not arranged in this neat hierarchy. Rather, life exhibits a messy interdependence, particularly as regards the issue of source. Every man, even Paul has to acknowledge, comes forth from a woman. Yet Paul is loath to see his analogy turned on its head (!), and so he steps back into a more characteristic theological affirmation: "all things come from God" (v. 12).

Woven throughout Paul's first argument, though, are the threads of a second one, spun out when the first argument founders. Paul was no cultural anthropologist, but he was a keen observer of the world. Knowing the unveiling of women to be wrong, he observes that women's hair is long (albeit up and covered), while men's is short. This, he deduces, is the natural state of affairs. Furthermore, he knows that shame attaches to the shaven head of a woman or the uncut hair of a man. Thus he bases his second argument on "nature" itself, that is, what is self-evidently "natural" according to his observation. He thus deduces that, since a woman's long hair covers her head, her head is meant to be covered and so should have a veil.

Note that Paul's observation of "nature" could have led to the opposite conclusion: a woman's long hair covers her head, and thus no additional veil is necessary. Again, these "proofs" function primarily, not to demonstrate the correctness of Paul's position against reasoned objections by determined opposition, but to reassure those who already acknowledged Paul's authority. This becomes even more evident in Paul's final justification for his position

(v. 16). Here he drops all pretense to argument and appeals boldly to custom, that is to say, "*We* don't do it that way." As anyone who has been on the receiving end of such a comment can attest, this is a conversation-ender, a clear signal that the speaker is summoning his or her (presumed) authority to terminate further discussion.

This text, then, has potential implications for the appropriate grounds of authority in the church and for appropriate and inappropriate sources of theological justification, as well as for the obvious issue of the concern for propriety in worship. All of these are significant issues for today's church. In this text, moreover, Paul shows himself to be a cultural traditionalist. Significantly, though, the issue in this text is *not* whether a woman is or is not to lead in worship. Indeed, the whole discussion is based on the assumption that women will lead. The text considers the conditions that should be placed on her leadership—conditions that, it should be noted, have to do with appearance rather than function.

This is not to say that this text is not involved in exercising greater control over women who lead in worship than over men who perform similar roles. The text betrays an underlying suspicion of women's dangerous sexuality, a suspicion that seems to be grounded in a fear of *difference*. But it is worth noting that this fear of difference, which we have seen from Paul elsewhere, does not preclude the participation of women in worship. Rather, another foundational principle at work here mitigates Paul's distrust of difference and leads him to establish a set of rules that makes women's participation in worship possible. Paul, speaking theologically as he was accustomed to do, might call it the enabling power of the Holy Spirit. We might do well to follow Paul's lead here.

1 Corinthians 14:33b–36

Understanding the background of chapter 11 in this way, we turn to the very difficult text of 1 Corinthians 14:33b–36. The statement appears in the midst of a discussion of worship practices, particularly speaking in tongues, and the text is worth reciting in full:

> As in all the churches of the saints, the women/wives should keep silent in the churches; for they are not permitted to speak, but they are to be subject, as the law also says. And if anyone [of them] wishes to learn, let her ask her own husband at home; for it is disgraceful for a woman/wife to speak in church. Or did the word of God come from you? Or has it reached you alone? (author's translation)

On the face of it, and as it is often interpreted, this text would seem to prohibit any public speaking by women in the assembly, or at least by married women (the Greek *gyne* means either "woman" or "wife"). Yet to interpret the text this way would fly in the face of the assumptions held in chapter 11. How, then, do we make sense of this text? Interpreters have commonly advanced several options.

The passage exhibits some text-critical difficulties. Verse 33b is generally read as the introductory phrase of the sentence that follows in verse 34 but can be read with the rest of verse 33. In such a reading the example of "all the churches of the saints" is not part of the issue of women's speech. In some ancient manuscripts verses 34–35 appear at the end of the chapter rather than as in current editions. In other manuscripts, the verses are in their usual place but with a marginal notation indicating that the copyist knew of other manuscripts that placed the verses elsewhere. These verses clearly interrupt the flow of the argument, so that modern translations often place this section in parentheses to show the break. If these verses were omitted altogether, the chapter's argument would flow smoothly with no hint that anything was missing. This combination of text-critical evidence leads some interpreters to see the prohibition against women's speech as an interpolation, perhaps placed first in the margin of the text to bring 1 Corinthians more in line with the admonitions of 1 Timothy and then incorporated later into the text itself. According to this view, then, it is not Paul himself but his later interpreters who wish to prohibit women's speech.[14]

Other scholars disagree. They argue that, distasteful as it might be for modern scholars, Paul's intent is in fact to rein in the activities of the women prominent in the leadership of the Corinthian congregation. He thus strictly limits their participation in worship and redirects the practices of the church in which women play a vital role. A leading proponent of this view is Antoinette Clark Wire, who argues that the rhetoric of all of 1 Corinthians is directed toward making Paul's stance seem logical, natural, and true and toward discrediting the perspective of his opponents, the women prophets.[15]

Others who see this text as Paul's own words argue for a more limited application of them. Paul, they say, knew of specific situations in the Corinthian congregation (cf. 1 Cor. 1:11–12; 5:1–2; 2 Cor. 7:7–8). He also knew of a specific situation in which a particular group of women, quite possibly young wives with no previous contact with Christianity or Judaism, were disrupting the worship service by talking continually among themselves or interrupting the service to ask questions. The scenario is quite plausible. Girls married early, often with little knowledge of the world outside their childhood home, and were expected to leave their own family's gods behind and adopt the gods of their new husbands. Thus, these scholars contend, Paul is speaking of a particular group of women/wives who are not part of the church leadership, but who instead are hindering the congregation's worship. Paul orders them to keep silent and listen. If they need further instruction, they should discuss the matter with the husband at home, since religious instruction of the family was part of the husband/ father's task. Paul directs this group to keep silent until, presumably, they learn the congregation's traditions and practices. Thus these women will help preserve decorum in the worship services, just as the women who participate in worship leadership do by appropriate dress and head covering.[16]

Yet another option for reading this text is perhaps the most speculative, but also takes best account of some of the text's odd features. Verse 36 is a rather strongly emotional outburst that has, in most readings, no clear referent. The first word of each clause is typically read (as in the translation above) as the disjunctive particle "or,"[17] and implies, if somewhat vaguely, that Paul is referring dismissively to some other view than the one he has just presented. It is also entirely possible that the first word of the verse is to be read "truly, indeed."[18] The only difference is in an accent mark, which the ancient manuscripts lack. The final verse of the section, then, would read, "Indeed, did the word of God come from you, or has it reached you alone?" Such a sharp retort would suggest that Paul was reacting strongly to the Corinthians' perspective. But what is that perspective?

At various other points in 1 Corinthians, Paul indicates that he is responding to questions that have been directed to him, either by personal messenger (as 1 Cor. 1:11) or in writing (as 1 Cor. 7:1). As we have noted, many modern translations cast the statement in 7:1, "It is well for a man not to touch a woman," in quotation marks. Editors judge that these are, in fact, the Corinthians' own words, to which Paul proceeds to respond, agreeing in part but also modifying the Corinthians' stance in some important ways. Similarly, Paul is seen to quote Corinthian slogans in 8:1 and 8:4, qualifying the application of those slogans as they have to do with eating meat offered to idols. It is reasonable, then, to suspect that Paul quotes the Corinthians' correspondence elsewhere in 1 Corinthians as well. Some interpreters argue that 1 Corinthians 14:33b–35 is just such a quotation. The Corinthians, eager to justify their position, even cite "the Law" as support. Paul, however, has already made clear his position on the participation of women in worship (they should be properly veiled when they pray and prophesy) and responds to this Corinthian assertion with uncharacteristic brevity (but characteristic ardor): "What? Do you (perhaps implied, 'you men') think you control the word of God?" If this reading is correct, the church's tradition of reading this text would be a sad irony, putting in Paul's own mouth a view he vigorously rejects.[19]

All these proposals for reading 1 Corinthians 14:33b–36 have strengths and weaknesses. Interpolation theories would be much stronger if we had even one reliable ancient text in which this passage is not present, or if the best texts we have displaced the passage, but such is not the case. The assertion that "Paul meant what he said" makes it difficult to reconcile this text with 1 Corinthians 11, which, as we have seen, assumes women's participation in worship. Any particular reconstruction of the historical situation to which the text is a response must necessarily be somewhat speculative. If Paul is indeed quoting the Corinthians here, it seems to be a much larger quotation than any other in the letter. On the other hand, it is somewhat difficult to imagine Paul citing "the Law" as support in the manner that this text does. It is also difficult to make sense of the surprised and angry outburst that follows. While I am inclined to adopt the view that Paul is addressing two groups of women in 1 Corinthians—recognized leaders in chapter 11, disruptive chatterers in chapter 14—I recognize that scholarly consensus is building toward the acknowledgment of 14:33b–36 as an interpolation. Our reading of 1 Corinthians 14:33b–36, so often cited as evidence that Paul opposed the participation of women in the church, will finally be determined not by study of this text alone but also by larger conclusions we reach about Paul's attitudes toward women.

Leadership, Asceticism, and Women's Roles

Ross Kraemer points out, following the anthropologist Mary Douglas, that women tend to gain in status, sometimes even reaching status parity with men, in societies or groups in which traditional sex-linked divisions of labor (for women, childbearing, child rearing, and domestic duties) are invalidated.[20] The earliest Christian communities may be an example of such a society, since they expected Christ to return quite soon to bring the end of the age. Various comments in the Pauline literature (especially 1 Corinthians 7), as well as other evidence from early Christianity, make it clear that asceticism and the expectation of martyrdom were quite common, even the norm, in these groups. Thus Paul (who personally tends toward asceticism) and others occasionally feel compelled to make a case for the acceptability of marriage and childbearing. It may well be that Paul and other leaders have, at least in part, the survival and viability of the Christian communities, and thus of the Christian witness, in mind when they counsel traditional family structures. The clear effect, however, is to redirect women back into their traditional, gender-defined roles, away from the relative status parity of asceticism. Granted, the ascetic ideal was often profoundly misogynistic in its expression: the common understanding was that women by renouncing their sexuality cast off the hindrances and imperfections of their gender and became more perfect, that is, more male. Nonetheless, the effect in Christian communities was apparently that women were drawn to the ascetic life for the freedoms it granted them from the constraints of a gender-hierarchical society.[21]

2 Corinthians: Authority and Acting Like a Leader

From the canonical texts 1 and 2 Corinthians themselves we know that we do not have all the correspondence that passed between Paul and the Corinthian congregation. Missing, of course, is what the Corinthians wrote to Paul (cf. 1 Cor. 7:1), with the exception of brief quotations in Paul's letters. Nor do we have everything Paul wrote. In 1 Corinthians 5:9 he refers to a previous letter, in which he told the believers not to associate with immoral persons. Second Corinthians 2:3–4 speaks of a letter written "out of much distress and anguish of heart and with many tears." While some scholars argue that the body of these letters is included within 1 and 2 Corinthians, most agree that these represent a larger and longer exchange, of which we have a significant but incomplete portion.

When we move into 2 Corinthians, additional questions arise. Paul is capable of shifting topics and moods within his letters, sometimes seemingly suddenly. Still, 2 Corinthians appears more fragmented than most of Paul's writings, so that scholars tend to see at least two, and possibly three or more, letters represented there.[22] Second Corinthians 10—13, at least, seems to be a separate document, written under changed circumstances and with a different agenda than the first part of 2 Corinthians. In addition, 2 Corinthians 8 and 9, which discuss the collection for Jerusalem, may be separate "administrative letters,"[23] or may have been part of the same correspondence as 2 Corinthians 1—7.

Given the evidence of the letters we have, and the comments made in them, we can reconstruct a tentative outline of Paul's relationship with the congregation in Corinth. It appears that this is a congregation founded by Paul, although he claims that he did not baptize many of the members (1 Cor. 1:14–16). We do not know what other leaders played a part in its establishment. The conflicting loyalties evidenced in the first part of 1 Corinthians point to a more complicated founding story than Paul implies. Nonetheless, he considers himself this congregation's founder (1 Cor. 4:15) and assumes for himself the responsibility and authority for its continued leadership. After this founding, he left the congregation and subsequently wrote to them (1 Cor. 5:9) and received information from them. Prior to writing the letter we now know as 1 Corinthians, he received information both in writing (1 Cor. 7:1) and by personal report (1 Cor. 1:11) of problems and questions that had arisen in the congregation. Some of these conflicts, ‑‑ as we have seen, have to do with church practice and the theological positions that underlie that practice. Other conflicts are more directly questions of authority and leadership, and specifically the authority Paul holds in the congregation.

After the letter was delivered, apparently by Timothy (1 Cor. 4:17), Paul made a visit to the congregation in which the tensions between congregation members and the apostle erupted into open conflict (2 Cor. 2:1).[24] Paul left Corinth and wrote the "letter of tears" (2 Cor. 2:4; 7:8, 12). He changed his plans so as not to return for another visit (2 Cor. 1:15–16, 1:23–2:1), while waiting for the resolution of the conflict. The opening section of 2 Corinthians testifies that the issue was resolved in favor of those who supported Paul. Paul thus writes of the "consolation" he has received from the congregation (2 Cor. 1:3–7) and magnanimously urges that his former opponent be reincorporated into the membership (2 Cor. 2:8). Either at this occasion or soon afterward, he also writes at some length (2 Cor. 8—9) about the collection he has begun for the believers in Jerusalem, urging the Corinthians to follow the example of other congregations in generous and sacrificial giving.

At some later point, then, some new crisis arose between Paul and the Corinthian congregation, this time dealing much more directly with Paul's leadership role and apostolic authority. Paul's spirited defense of himself appears in 2 Corinthians 10—13.[25] Unfortunately, we do not know the outcome of this last missive from Paul. Perhaps, once again, his rhetoric was effective, and he was reaffirmed as the congregation's authority figure. On the other hand, we need to be careful not to retroject the later church's estimation of Paul as crucial leader and authority figure back into the period of the earliest congregations, many of which seem to have survived without Paul's guidance.

The Rhetoric of Weakness

In any case, it is worth paying close attention to the way Paul conducts himself in the highly impassioned, highly rhetorical 2 Corinthians 10—13. The situation seems to be this: Paul finds it necessary to confront rival leaders in Corinth, who have challenged Paul's authority with the congregation and sought to supplant it with their own. (Interestingly, nothing in this text identifies how the opponents' theology or morals differed from Paul's, although Paul seems to equate his own authority with the purity of the gospel; see 2 Cor. 11:2–4). The opponents apparently made grandiose claims for their spiritual power (which they seemed to be able to substantiate with the Corinthians) and denigrated Paul by comparison. It seems, as well, that they required fees for their teaching and other services, whereas Paul supported himself and received support from other congregations during his Corinthian sojourns. The opponents suggested that what they had to offer was therefore more valuable: "you get what you pay for." Paul calls (2 Cor. 11:5; 12:11) them "super-apostles" (*oi hyperlian apostoloi*) in biting satire. He deflates their practice of commendation by commending himself for behaviors that would be seen as scarcely commendable.

Paul's syntax, which is often less than straightforward, becomes even more convoluted in these chapters as he rants against his opponents. He calls himself a "fool" (11:16), "weak" (11:21), and a "madman" (11:23), and insists that he will "boast" (11:18) as his opponents do while simultaneously insisting that "boasting" is of no use. His "boast," however, is in his "weakness" (11:30—12:10), as he recounts his sufferings and humiliations. All the while, though, Paul does not back down at all on what he asserts as the established fact of his authority (10:8). At the end of the passage he once again affirms that he will come and set things right in the congregation (13:2, 10). The tone throughout this section is emotional rather than rational, hysterical rather than reasoned. That means that in the dualistic thought world occupied by Paul and his conversation partners, Paul is behaving like a woman.

So what is going on here? One possible interpretation is to surmise that Paul has "lost his cool," that these are angry ramblings without further significance. Another is to suggest that he is playing the "fool" in the sense of the well-established stock dramatic character, the one who defies certain behavioral conventions to be able to say what no one else is able to say. I tend to think that we should see in this emotional outburst the careful rhetorical work of a seasoned practitioner. Paul is rhetorically fashioning an argument, angry though he might be. He chooses a way to present himself to his Corinthian correspondents that he calculates is the most likely to bring them around to his way of thinking. And the way he chooses to persuade them in 2 Corinthians 10—13 is to defy cultural expectations and fight, not just like a "fool," but like a woman.

I do not intend to imply that Paul consciously and consistently chose to identify himself in a womanly or effeminate fashion by his hysterical self-presentation or by his appeals to weakness and foolishness. Indeed, at various points Paul casts himself in culturally significant masculine roles, as when he images himself as the *paterfamilias* to his Corinthian children (2 Cor. 6:13; 11:2–3; 12:14). Nonetheless his self-identification with weakness, humiliation, and suffering connect him with what would have been understood in his own context as feminine qualities. Such qualities would be viewed as unsuitable for one whose rhetorical claims to be worthy of a hearing ought to be backed up by a presentation of power and control—that is, of manliness.[26] Paul's rhetorical claim, of course, is that the difference between his opponents and himself is one of human versus divine perception. His strategy, though, was a risky one. As Jennifer Larson notes, he "may have found resistance from some male converts to the idea of 'strength in weakness,' because weakness was so strongly associated with femininity."[27]

More significant for us, though, than speculation on whether Paul himself was conscious of the "femininity" of his rhetorical self-presentation is the wedge that such a self-presentation drives—*particularly* in a society that equates gender roles so closely with personal traits—between the "naturalness" of gender-defined roles and the possibility of imaging leadership differently. Paul's rhetorical opponents in 2 Corinthians saw weakness as servile and effeminate. Paul sees it as reflective of divine rather than human power. I recognize that Paul may not have himself recognized the implications of such a claim for the place of women as well as men in the leadership of this new, divinely constituted community. Indeed, I suspect that he did not, since on other occasions (e.g., 1 Cor. 11:3–9) he seems to reinforce rather than undermine traditional gender hierarchy. Nonetheless, we can choose to explore Paul's presentation of "power in weakness" as one of the growing edges of Paul's theology, a place where his thought stretches toward a truly new way of being human in Christ, a way of being beyond gender division. But that is a topic for another chapter.

CHAPTER 4

No Male and Female

Paul's letter to the Galatians is a particularly interesting study in the dynamic of constructed masculinity, as we noted earlier. Paul writes as if male readers are the norm. He speaks to "you" who are considering circumcision. No female colleagues or church members are mentioned in the letter. The only woman named is Hagar, in the context of a particularly convoluted allegorical interpretation. Male body language is prevalent throughout, with frequent references to foreskin, circumcision, and sperm, and one comment about castration. "Even the gospel itself is linked to male anatomy, with Paul coining the two rather striking phrases 'gospel of the foreskin' and 'gospel of the circumcision' (2:7), which are repeated nowhere else in the New Testament."[1] Yet, at the very center of Paul's argument in Galatians, we find the famous passage often called the "Magna Carta of Christian equality." Galatians 3:28 states that "there is neither Jew nor Greek, there is neither slave nor free, there is no male and female; for all of you are one in Christ Jesus" (author's translation). What are we to make of this text, and how do we interpret it in light of the letter? Then, what do we make of Galatians in our larger understanding of Paul?

"No Male and Female"

Galatians 3:27–28 is now widely recognized as a liturgical formula that Paul quotes in his argument. The imagery, and likely the original setting, is that of baptism, with its powerful imagery of new birth. Later in the history of the church and very likely already in Paul's day, candidates disrobed for baptism. Then, wet and naked like a newborn, they were clothed in identical, plain, probably white, robes. As everyday clothing was an important marker of status, the identical robes would reinforce the last line of the liturgy: "all of you are one in Christ Jesus" (cf. v. 27: you "have clothed yourselves with Christ"). In this new state, the liturgy proclaims, old distinctions are gone. Ethnicity, social rank, even gender do not exist. Only oneness "in Christ" matters.

Paul reminds the Galatians of something they already know, using words they had first heard at the solemn and joyous occasion of their own baptism. These words had been reinforced by repetition of the ritual as new members were added to the congregation. While Paul may have added some phrases as he cites the liturgy in his letter, the tradition was likely this:

For you are all sons of God in Christ Jesus;
(28a)   There is no Jew nor Greek,
(28b)   There is no slave nor free,
(28c)   There is no male and female.
(28d)   For you are all one in Christ Jesus.
                    (Author's translation)

What did this proclamation mean? Was it an expression of fervent eschatological hope, that in some future day God would bring about such a reordering of society? Or did the earliest Christians understand their baptism to mean a different way of living in community in the here and now? Wayne Meeks has argued persuasively that this text, in its original baptismal context, should be understood as a "performative utterance," shaping the symbolic universe of the group of believers by its proclamation. "So long as it is spoken validly, as perceived within that community's accepted norms of order, it does what it says."[2]

No doubt these small communities of believers understood full well that racial, economic, and gender status markers still mattered in the larger world of which they were a part. Still, the baptismal proclamation declared that, within the community, these distinctions no longer held; they were, instead, "all one in Christ Jesus."

We have already seen that first-century Greco-Roman society was highly, and often rigidly, stratified. Race, economic class, and gender mattered, as well as wealth, family connections, citizenship, and a host of other factors that interacted to determine one's place in society. We have noted, too, that early believers often experienced what Meeks has called "status inconsistency," that is, they had both "high" and "low" status markers (wealthy women, for example, or free Greek men whose client status placed them on a par with slaves). The declaration that these markers of status were nullified in the Christian community did more than resolve members' psychological tensions. It also envisioned an entirely different way of perceiving themselves and one another and of understanding their responsibilities to each other within a community structured on such principles.

But what, specifically, about the phrase "no male and female"? Is it different, somehow, than the other two sets of contrasts? Our social location might lead us quickly to answer that it is undoubtedly so, given our relative economic mobility and increasingly prevalent attitudes of racial equality. Gender is different, we might argue, because it is rooted in biological differences, in the differences between male and female bodies. Such an argument, though, fails to take account of the important distinction between biological sex and gender, as well as the difference between our way of understanding sexual difference and that of Paul and his contemporaries (see chapter 1). Sex (whether on a one-sex or two-sex model) has to do with the body's reproductive equipment, but gender is a *social* category. Gender constructs expectations and mores on society's *perceptions* of the difference that biological difference makes. As we have seen, in the ancient world gender was perceived *less* as biological difference than as difference in one's social roles and behaviors. The distinction between male and female, then, is not inherently different from the distinction between Jew and Greek or slave and free. All have to do with categories over which the individual has no control, and all are given meaning by the way society perceives and structures those categories.

In this context, "no male and female," however, *does* bring something different. Its grammatical structure breaks the neat parallelism of the preceding two phrases. Each contrasting pair is introduced with the words *ouk eni*, "there is no": the Jew/Greek pair and the slave/free pair are linked with the conjunction *oude*, "nor," commonly paired with *ouk* in the sense "neither/nor." The last pair, though, uses *kai*, "and," rather than *oude*. Also, instead of "man and woman," as might be expected, the phrase is "male and female." Such variations from the established pattern, and from likely expectations, prompt us to look and listen more carefully to this text and discern what else might be going on.

What we hear, and what the earliest Christians are likely to have heard as well, attentive to scripture as they were, is an echo of Genesis 1:27: "Male and female he created them." The Greek text in the Septuagint is *arsen kai thely*, identical to Galatians 3:28. The baptismal liturgy, then, recalls the narrative of creation and brings to mind the created order. The liturgy implies that this created order is overturned or reordered "in Christ." Greeks no less than Jews would have sensed that the dependable structure of the cosmos relied on the existence of pairs of opposites. Aristotle's *Metaphysics* cites the Pythagorean Table of Opposites, which includes among others the pair "male and female."[3] Still, the use of the phrase in this text probably resonated most strongly with the Christian community in their familiarity with scripture and the creation narrative. This created order, this structure, is set aside "in Christ." Implied here, but not yet stated, is the new creation Christ is bringing about in the believing community and in the world.

Understanding the Text in Its Original Context

The understanding of this text as part of a baptismal liturgy echoing Genesis 1:27 provides us with a rare and important insight into some very early Christian communities at a crucial moment in their lives. We view them as they incorporate new members into the body of Christ. At that moment they proclaimed a fundamental restructuring of the cosmos. This restructuring must have had implications not only for their standing before God but also for their relationships as members of the community so reordered. What, precisely, it meant to live in such a community is impossible to discern. Elisabeth Schüssler Fiorenza notes that membership in the Christian community would have meant surrender of multiple privileges for the members of highest status, since heads of household (who would have been master *and* husband *and* father) would relinquish their power over social subordinates, as well as their social privileges. She also contends that to live as "no male and female" would mean the end of marriage. She writes, "as such, Galatians 3:28c does not assert that there are no longer men and women in Christ, but that patriarchal marriage—and sexual relationships between male and female—is no longer constitutive of the new community in Christ."[4]

Others argue for a less radical understanding of the text. They suggest that it does not rule out marriage but that it does make singleness spiritually acceptable for women by disconnecting their status before God from their role in the family structure.[5] Still others have claimed that, in at least some early Christian groups, "no male and female" was understood as a complete erasure of sexual difference. This belief resulted in the complete breakdown of hierarchy and in enforced celibacy or libertinism—outcomes that seem to underlie the factionalism Paul confronted in the Corinthian congregation.[6] What the liturgy almost certainly did *not* mean, though, was a change in believers' individual status "before God" that had *no* implications for the community so ordered. As Schüssler Fiorenza summarizes, "Gal 3:28 is therefore best understood as a communal Christian self-definition rather than a statement about the baptized individual. It proclaims that in the Christian community all distinctions of religion, race, class, nationality, and gender are insignificant."[7]

Understanding the Text in Its Pauline Context

But what the earliest Christian communities understood their baptismal liturgy to mean is one thing; what it means when Paul cites it in the context of Galatians may be quite another. Many scholars argue that Paul's use of the liturgy is quite at odds with its original significance. One commentator notes wryly, "Feminist and liberation oriented readings rather commonly have treated the baptismal formula of Gal. 3:26–28 as a kind of *ET*, a lovely lonely alien unhappily trapped in the hostile matter of a Pauline letter."[8] Baptism is clearly not the main issue in Paul's letter to the Galatians. This is the letter's only explicit reference to baptism.

On first impression it seems that Paul uses the baptismal formula in his argument simply because the first pair of the three reinforces his own point. Similarly, a preacher today might quote a few lines of a familiar hymn, even though only one line or image from the hymn is pertinent to the sermon. Indeed, it is this "imperfect fit" of the liturgy into its present rhetorical context that persuades many interpreters that the text is traditional material and not Paul's own composition. This way of reading Galatians 3:28 in context minimizes the importance of the text, and in particular the phrase "no male and female," in Paul's theology. In this view, "no male and female" becomes something of a "throwaway line," bearing little significance for our understanding of Paul's presentation of God's saving work.

To this reading Daniel Boyarin responds with characteristic incisiveness: "If Paul took 'no Jew or Greek' as seriously as all of Galatians attests that he clearly did, how could he possibly—unless he is incoherent or a hypocrite—not have taken 'no male and female' with equal seriousness?"[9] Boyarin has his own reservations about Paul's theological agenda, reading it as a dualistic spirit-flesh hierarchy that values unity as sameness and results in the devaluing of physical difference. Whether or not one adopts all of Boyarin's perspective, though, his objection here is certainly well taken. It is inappropriate simply to dismiss this text as an unintentional aside. The seriousness of Paul's argument demands that we pay closer attention.

Another way to read Galatians 3:28 in context is to speculate that Paul cites the baptismal liturgy in full, including the "no male and female" line, precisely to bring it into the scope of his theological project and thereby to stifle other interpretations of the liturgy. To follow this line of thinking is, of course, to look for other Pauline texts that address the same topics as Galatians 3:28 and to read them as Paul's exegesis of the baptismal formula. First Corinthians 7 is often cited in this regard. One commentator calls it "Paul's authentic commentary" on Galatians 3:28 and claims that, "In so doing, he understands the schema of our concepts in an astonishingly conservative fashion precisely as an argument for the status quo." In this view 1 Corinthians 7 anticipates an imminent end of this world, so that its counsels seem to be based in part on the conviction that the present order is not worth changing.[10] Others compare Galatians 3:28 not only with 1 Corinthians 7 but also with the references to women in 1 Corinthians 11 and 14 and with the issue of slavery underlying Philemon. They see Galatians 3:28 as either proclamation of a spiritual status that does not completely hold in the physical realm or as an ideal as yet unreached, or perhaps even unreachable, in the present fallen cosmos.[11]

This method of reading takes us beyond a single text into a wider consideration of Paul's theology. We are well aware that Paul contends, often forcefully, for his interpretations of scripture, tradition, and God's saving act in Christ over against other interpretations. Paul opposed both enforced celibacy and sexual libertinism,[12] either of which could logically have followed from a proclamation of "no male and female." Later, gnostic and ascetic Christian groups in the second and third centuries understood salvation as a return to a state of androgynous perfection, "no male and female."[13] Paul almost certainly would have been aware of interpretations of the Genesis narrative that envisioned a state of primal androgyny. Paul's contemporary Philo, for example, explains the creation of Adam in Genesis 2 this way. Yet while Paul presents Christ as the fulfillment of which Adam was the type (e.g., in Romans 5), he neither cites the tradition of the androgyne nor draws the conclusion that being "in Christ" means the diminishing of sexual differentiation. Rather, we see that quite the opposite is the case, as in his tortured argument in 1 Corinthians 11 where he uses "natural" differences between male and female to advocate women's head coverings. Perhaps, then, we should read Galatians 3:28 in its Pauline context as Paul's effort to "tame" a "dangerous" traditional liturgical text. Our exegetical response, then, is either to reignite its "dangerous" nature, believing full well that we are acting contrary to Paul's intention when we do so, or else to follow Paul's lead and insist on parsing such texts carefully, knowing that otherwise they can lead to theological mischief.

Is there yet another way to read Galatians 3:28 in context? We must recognize that, however good we may become at psychological exegesis, we ultimately do not have access to the mind of Paul or of any other ancient writer. More than that, though, a faithful stance toward the biblical texts does not require that we focus our task solely on the text's meaning in its original context—to do so is, as Krister Stendahl has so aptly put it, "a nostalgic attempt to play 'First Century.'"[14] But neither are we at liberty to read into the text any meaning we wish. Rather, a faithful approach to Galatians 3:28, as to any biblical text, involves careful analysis of the text and the ideas, images, and metaphors that it calls forth, and then considered reflection on these data to discern what they might say for us today.

"All Sons, All One"

How might this approach unfold with regard to Galatians 3:28? A first move is to consider carefully the immediate context into which the liturgy is set in Paul's letter. Verses 26–29 read as follows:

> For you are all sons of God through the faith in Christ Jesus;
> for as many of you as were baptized in Christ have clothed yourselves with Christ.
> There is no Jew nor Greek,
> There is no slave nor free,
> There is no male and female;
> For you are all one [masc. sing.] in Christ Jesus.
> And if you are Christ's, then you are seed of Abraham, heirs according to the promise. (Author's translation)

On first reading this context does not look promising for a liberative reading of "no male and female." Indeed, the believers are called "sons" (*uioi*) and "seed" (*sperma*), incorporated into a "one" (*heis*) that is grammatically masculine. They hear that that they are "heirs" (*kleronomoi*) in a legal system of male inheritance. "No male and female" is beginning to sound like "no female—only male."

But it is also possible to read the masculine grammatical constructions and male metaphors in this passage as pointing to a reality that is, indeed, beyond the divide between male and female—even though that division is inscribed in the very language in which the text is written. "You are all one," Paul writes (or quotes). You are not one *thing* (which would be implied by the neuter form of the Greek word "one"), but one *person*. Here it begins to dawn that "the body of Christ" is not simply a convenient occasional metaphor for Paul. In a real sense the conception of the church as a body, a *person*, an organic, diverse, and living whole, runs deep through Paul's theologizing about the church and his understanding of life "in Christ." If we were "one," *hen* (neuter), we would be one *thing*—all alike. Then our value would be in our sameness. But we are one *person*, expressed in Greek by the grammatically masculine *heis*. As one person we are not to model sameness ("If the whole body were an eye, where would the hearing be?" [1 Cor. 12:17]) but diversity, mutuality, and interdependence. The grammar may be gender-exclusive, but the image it invites us to imagine reaches beyond generic sameness to a celebration of diverse mutuality.

Sonship and Inheritance

Similarly, the language of "sons" and "heirs" speaks to a society in which the legal status of sonship was very different from the reality of being a daughter. Paul's larger argument, in this part of Galatians, is not about men and women, not even about sons and daughters, but about sons and non-sons—in the sense of inheritance. In those days, long before the advent of DNA testing, there was no need for it. Sonship was a legal matter, not a biological one. What mattered was not sex (either the act or the organs) but status. One man could, theoretically (and sometimes actually), father children by several women. Only certain of these would be his sons, in the sense that they would be entitled to receive an upbringing from their father or hold claim to his property after his death. A man could have male offspring but no sons—indeed, it would be possible for a man to adopt his own biological offspring as a legal son. "Sons" became "heirs" when they were born or adopted. The death of the father gave them *control* of the property that had been theirs all along, because they held the status of sons.[15]

In an odd sense, then, everything depended on the mother—not her ability to bear children, but her legal status vis-à-vis the man whose child she bore. If she were his wife (a status only available to free women), her male children were his sons. If she were a slave, a mistress, a domestic partner to whom the categories of marriage did not apply (as was the case with slave unions), the male offspring were not sons. Then their well-being and their future would have depended on the choices of those who had power over them—the mother, to some extent; the person (father, husband, master, etc.) who was the mother's legal guardian; the biological father, to the extent of his resources and willingness to acknowledge them; and those to whom the biological father might be obligated (master, patron, and so forth).

Being a "son" also meant that one would become, eventually, a legally responsible adult. The status of "daughter" did not have the same legal ramifications, since women were legally "minors"—under the legal control of another—all their lives. Moreover, the status of "son" would have mattered little legally without an estate to inherit. If, as has often been argued, the lower strata of society comprised the bulk of Paul's congregations, then for males and females alike the promise of "adoption as sons" would sound as a word of hope, beyond the reality of their present physical circumstances. Freedom, responsibility, investment with an inheritance—all these can only be promised to believers through the gender-exclusive metaphor of sonship.

Yet, as Elisabeth Schüssler Fiorenza has stated, "The text uses this metaphor in order to profile the freedom, inheritance, and independence of the new status of baptized persons as 'sons.'"[16] In Christ God offers all persons—Jew or Greek, slave or free, male or female—the privileged status that can only be described as "sons of God."

Persistent Tensions

Yet an honest reading of Galatians must admit that all is still not well. Despite Paul's restatement and expansion of a ringing proclamation of equality in Christ, of incorporation into a single body of diverse members and of adoption as free and responsible agents, Paul himself exhibits practices of division and exclusion. His rhetorical arsenal includes silencing, othering, and downright ridicule of those with whom he disagrees. The fact that we do not know the identity of the rival preachers against whom Paul argues in Galatians, nor the positive points of their message, comes from Paul's manner of referring to them. Rather than identifying his opponents by terms they might use to describe themselves, he refers to them as those who proclaim another (unnamed) gospel. By so speaking, he pronounces a curse on them from the very beginning of his argument (1:9; cf. 4:17, 6:12). He is not willing to acknowledge any possibility that his opponents' motives might be genuine. Rather, he characterizes them as "false believers, secretly brought in,…to spy on the freedom we have in Christ Jesus" (2:4). Clearly, the rival preachers' message includes the necessity of circumcision for the Galatian males. On this point Paul employs *double entendre* on the word "cut." "You who want to be justified by the law have cut yourselves off from Christ," he argues (5:4), and in an even more sarcastic tone, "I wish the ones who trouble you would cut themselves off!" (5:12, author's translation). Appropriate to the subject or not, this sounds more like schoolyard taunt than reasoned theological discussion.

Nor are the Galatians themselves spared the barb of Paul's ire. He addresses them as "foolish," claims that they have been "bewitched" (3:1–3), and says, in an apparent attempt to shame them, "I am afraid that my work for you may have been wasted" (4:11). Such patterns of argumentation stand in ironic contrast to Paul's own counsel, "if anyone is detected in a transgression, you who have received the Spirit should restore such a one in a spirit of gentleness" (6:1). The mode of argument, as Elizabeth Castelli has pointed out, is "relentlessly dualistic and oppositional."[17]

In addition, the pronouncement of "no longer slave or free" in 3:28 finds disconcerting contrast in the Sarah and Hagar allegory of 4:22–31. This text presents slavery and freedom as permanent states, not only for individuals but in some sense for their descendants as well. In addition it pronounces judgment based on the inequality of the slave and free conditions. Paul reinscribes the differences of social class and status between Sarah and Hagar so that they represent not merely the differences of circumstance between two human beings but the essential differences between "us," the "in-group," and "them," those who are seen as "on the outs" with God. Indeed, the image trades on the legal definition of sonship (and descendance from Abraham) to make its point. Of Galatians 3:28, Castelli asks, "What does it mean to invoke such a formula (which on its face seems to imply a radical dissolution of socially constructed differences) when the rest of the argument in whose service the formula is invoked is predicated on precisely the same oppositions one claims to be undoing through ritual?"[18] We may argue that Paul's allegory is constructed for a specific purpose according to the interpretive conventions of his time and that the social structures and gendered identities behind the story it uses allegorically are not at issue. Still, Paul's use of the story may indicate that he has not yet banished the notion of social inequality from his thinking. The answer to Castelli's insightful question must take account of the complexity and tension in the letter to the Galatians.

Interpretive Options

It is not *necessary* to read this text as an internalizing or spiritualizing of equality and a reinscription of social patriarchy. It is also possible to read Galatians as the struggle to articulate the act of God in Jesus Christ—an act so strikingly radical that even its quite articulate interpreters, like Paul, speak of it haltingly and inconsistently. Krister Stendahl identifies the problem as a gap between Paul's "theological rapture" and his willingness or ability to make it a reality in his society. "I happen to think Paul was a better theologian than implementer…It seems that he saw a vision, but he did not know quite how to implement it fully."[19] Daniel Boyarin argues that Paul made a considered choice. "He did not think this new creation could be entirely achieved on the social level *yet*. Some of the program was already possible; some would have to wait."[20] Bonnie Thurston emphasizes the experience of struggle: "What I, personally, see in Paul as he is reflected in his letters is a man in process, a person struggling to understand the full implications of what God has done in Jesus and what, specifically, that means for him. Paul was living the tension between what had *been* his tradition and what was coming to *be* his tradition."[21]

However we may speculate on Paul's own attitude, though, our interpretation should focus on the radical nature of what Mary Ann Tolbert has called "an act of outrageous inclusivity." For Paul himself, this meant primarily the incorporation of persons of diverse racial and ethnic backgrounds into the covenant relationship between God and Abraham and the Jewish people.[22] Such a radical change could not be casually or simply explained or incorporated. Indeed, believers in Paul's tradition continue to seek its full implementation even today.

Such a monumental change, as Paul well understood, could not be implemented simply by making the covenant between God and the Jewish people wider, by incorporating Gentiles as Jewish converts, as his opponents in Galatia apparently intended. Neither is this a case of Paul, a free Jewish male who already knows he has access to God, graciously opening the doors and saying, Greeks, you may come in as if you were Jews. Slaves, you may come in as if you were free. Females, you may come in as if you were males. Rather, I want to argue that what Paul is struggling toward is what he writes in Galatians 3:28. The divisions *no longer hold*. Human beings have, as it were, started from scratch. Beverly Gaventa expresses it well when she says that the gospel, in Galatians, is an invading force that "necessarily obliterates worlds," including the world of the Law, but also other "worlds" in which persons identify themselves by ethnicity, social standing, and gender. "The only location available for those grasped by the gospel is 'in Christ.'"[23]

The Order of New Creation

Appropriately, Paul not only trumps the Judaizers' argument of connection to God through the Mosaic law and circumcision with an argument of connection to God through the promise to Abraham (Gal. 3:17); he also traces that connection back even further in sacred history, to reestablish the relationship between God and humanity from its beginning point. The regression can be seen in the baptismal formula itself, with its references to

- Jew/Greek—the Abraham story of Genesis 12, although admittedly the name "Greek" is anachronistic;
- slave/free—slavery is first mentioned in the Bible in Genesis 9 in the narrative of the sons of Noah; and finally
- male and female—first mentioned in the creation narrative, Genesis 1:27.

Far from being a thoughtless quotation, Paul's citation of "no male and female," with the reference to Genesis 1:27 that it includes, brings to the surface a theme that runs like a subterranean river through the letter to the Galatians. This theme forms the convictional basis for Paul's argument throughout the letter. Paul is persuaded that God's act in Christ Jesus has not merely brought the era of the Law to its completion, significant though that may be. Rather, that act in Christ signals no less than the end of the world as we know it and the establishment of an entirely new order. This new order stands under divine control, as was the previous order, and thus has some things in common with it. Nonetheless, this order is entirely new. At the end of the letter to the Galatians, Paul summarizes this theme by referring to this grounding conviction with characteristic brevity: "For neither circumcision nor uncircumcision is anything; but a new creation is everything!" (Gal. 6:15). In the next chapter we will explore further Paul's notion of "new creation" to see how its expression and promise shapes Paul's theological thinking.

As the early chapters of Galatians make clear, Paul understood his own calling to be specifically a mission to the Gentiles. (See esp. Gal. 1:16.) He took this specific calling very seriously. Thus it is not necessary to assume that Paul is only concerned with the "Jew nor Greek" part of the baptismal formula. Rather, as Daniel Boyarin has suggested, it makes more sense to infer the opposite.[24] Paul took all of the proclamation's abolitions of division with utmost seriousness. *His* calling, however, was to proclaim Christ among the Gentiles. This remained his clearest and most consistent focus throughout his ministry. His commitment to "no slave nor free" and "no male and female" is more ambiguously expressed in his ministry and writings because it was less in his theological focus. Such lack of focus came not by his own choice but by his calling.

Paul's use of scripture may serve as an instructive example of his commitment to the Gentile mission. As Amy Plantinga Pauw notes, Gentiles, like women, are scantily represented in Israel's scriptures. "Convinced nonetheless of their full inclusion in God's promises, Paul did not hesitate to pry open some space for them in the biblical texts, even when this required what must have appeared to be profound discontinuities with established interpretive traditions."[25]

Pauw goes on to note that Paul rarely reads women into a scriptural text. So what happens if we take Paul's vigorous inclusion of Gentiles as a pattern rather than reading it as a circumscription? What if, instead of seeing Paul as one who proclaims ethnic inclusion but chooses to let economic and gender divisions stand, we take Paul as someone who demonstrates intense focus on his particular calling from God? If we read Paul this way, we can believe that God calls some persons, even ourselves, specifically to ministries of economic or gender inclusiveness the way Paul was called as apostle to the Gentiles. Then Paul becomes not a deterring force but a model. He is a limited, human model, to be sure, as all human beings are limited—by time and place, by historical and cultural blindnesses. But the biblical witness, including the letters of Paul, is that God uses human beings to achieve bits and pieces of the divine purpose. If, in this, Paul provides us an example, then we are all the richer for the witness of his letters.

CHAPTER 5

Paul the Iconoclast

Thus far we have acknowledged that Paul was a man of his own time. He consciously addressed women only when they differed from the male "norm." He quite likely believed (at least at some level) that female bodies were constituted of a different substance than male bodies. He could not imagine a society in which women were not under male control—even while he worked with women who managed their own affairs and contributed to the leadership of the earliest Christian congregations. Ought we still hold out any hope at all that this man Paul has anything worthwhile to say to us?

On the other hand, we see in Paul a man with heightened concerns for his own authority and limited by the socially stratified society in which he lived. Despite all this, he was willing to use female images for himself—the woman in labor, the nursing mother—and to present himself as having the "feminine" characteristics of foolishness and emotionalism. This man matter-of-factly acknowledged the accomplishments of women in the same work in which he himself engaged. We see a man who, due in part no doubt to his eschatological expectations, offered countercultural advice for women to remain unmarried. With this advice, however, he pointed to a higher loyalty for women than simply to a husband and to a husband's family.

Paul boldly stated an exegetical principle of undifferentiation by race, class, or gender. Then in one of those aspects—the aspect of race, Jew and Gentile—he argued for this undifferentiation in ways that brought him into conflict even with other members of his own new religious movement. This Paul was a zealous, stubborn, committed iconoclast. He firmly believed that God had done something new in the world in the person of Jesus the Christ. Those of us who share his faith, even if we disagree with some of his stances, may do well to attend to his manner of proclaiming it.

An Approach to Paul's Theology

Scholars have written heavy tomes on Paul's theology. Plenty of academicians stay busy with the project of ascertaining the right way even to *approach* Paul's theology. A Pauline systematic theology, collecting what Paul said about the various topics typically treated in a systematic study, seems to have the virtue of thoroughness. Still, such a collection hardly does justice to Paul the occasional theologian. Paul wrote to specific congregations about specific issues. He did *not* organize his own thinking along what we think of as systematic lines.

Should we take one of Paul's letters and follow its outlines and categories? Romans seems a good candidate, being generally deemed Paul's most explicit and sustained theological argument. But what, then, of the topics that Paul does not treat in Romans, but that show up elsewhere in his letters? Are they simply woven in wherever they seem to be relevant without regard for the integrity of their original contexts? Or should we perhaps stick them in an appendix? A recent decade-long effort engaged a number of Pauline scholars in the project of articulating Paul's theology by considering the smaller letters first, then progressing to Galatians, the Corinthian correspondence, and finally Romans. (Interestingly, this group reached the end of their quite productive project not only without consensus on Paul's theology but also continuing to disagree on what exactly they were seeking and whether it could, in fact, be found.[1])

A "Center" for Pauline Theology

Significantly, several of the scholars involved in this project noted that one set of ideas arose with noticeable frequency in their discussions. The concept, first articulated by J. Christiaan Beker, suggests that Paul's theology is to be located in the "hermeneutical interaction between the coherent center of the gospel and its contingency."[2] Beker insists that the relationship of "coherence" to "contingency" is not simply that of principle to application, but that the dynamic itself is essential to understanding Paul. Nonetheless, he argues vigorously for a "center" or "core" of Paul's theology, which he understands to be the apocalyptic "coming triumph of God." Even more than Beker's specific proposals about the essentially apocalyptic nature of Paul's theology, this notion of a dynamic center or core has captured the imagination of other Pauline scholars. Thus much of the discussion of Pauline theology today regards finding and articulating that "center" from which Paul speaks, or in Paul's own terms the "truth of the gospel" (Gal. 2:5, 14).

This way of proceeding has much to commend it. It seeks to take account of Paul's own priorities by weighting the issues with which he seems to have been most concerned, yet it makes room for the very different ways he speaks to and theologizes with different congregations. Too, I tend to agree with Beker that Paul's eschatological horizon is an important factor to consider when seeking to discern his theology. Paul's sense that the triumph of God is both certain and soon to come orders his priorities. It also contributes to what has frequently been termed an "interim ethic," a way of living that makes most sense if it is understood to be for the short term and the present company, rather than for succeeding generations. This is not, however, simply to say that Paul's theology is founded on the belief, which turned out to be mistaken, that Christ would return to earth soon to take his church out of the present world. Rather, in Beker's formulation, Paul understands what God has done in Christ to be the first act of God's bringing about the final divine triumph over the world's forces of evil. This statement is, of necessity, rather general, but it is an apt summary of much of what is most important to Paul's understanding of the gospel. Unpacking it brings us close to much of what Paul emphasizes in his presentation of God's work in Christ.

"In Christ" Theology

A theology of Paul needs to take into account several other important factors. One is Paul's characteristic way of describing believers and churches as "in Christ" (*en Christo*). This phrase appears fifty-two times in the undisputed letters. At times it seems simply to be an alternative to the adjective "Christian."[3] For example, in Romans 16:7 Andronicus and Junia are described as "prominent among the apostles, and they were *in Christ* before I was" (italics added for emphasis). Galatians 1:22 speaks of "the churches of Judea that are *in Christ*"—perhaps more literally (although awkward in English) "the in-Christ churches." Other texts use "in Christ" or "in Christ Jesus" to describe the divine work: "redemption…in Christ Jesus" (Rom. 3:24), "eternal life in Christ Jesus our Lord" (Rom. 6:23), "sanctified in Christ Jesus" (1 Cor. 1:2), and so forth. Still other texts seem to point with this theological shorthand toward a much more important concept, a participation with Christ in God's saving work. Several key Pauline texts include the phrase:

> "So if anyone is *in Christ*, there is a new creation: everything old has passed away; see, everything has become new!" (2 Cor. 5:17).

> "There is no longer Jew or Greek, there is no longer slave or free, there is no longer male and female; for all of you are one *in Christ Jesus*" (Gal. 3:28).

> "And the peace of God, which surpasses all understanding, will guard your hearts and your minds *in Christ Jesus*" (Phil. 4:7) (italics added for emphasis).

The prominence of this phrase, and the apparently significant relationship which it signals, led Albert Schweitzer, early in the twentieth century, to speak of Paul's "eschatological mysticism of the Being-in-Christ."[4] Since then scholars have considered how "in Christ" signals a mystical side of Paul's theology or a participatory element in his understanding of the relationship between believers and Christ.

Closely related to this is Paul's repeated discussion of believers as the "body of Christ." This is, after all, a metaphorical rephrasing of the idea of being "in Christ." As a metaphor of an already enigmatic phrase, "body of Christ" opens all sorts of interpretive possibilities but does little to point us to a definitive interpretation. First Corinthians 12 is the lengthiest exposition of the metaphor. Here Paul emphasizes the variety of functions of the parts of the physical body (eye for seeing, ear for hearing, and so on) to demonstrate the need for a variety of functions by members of the congregation. Apparently, Paul wants to short-circuit some members' claims to superiority of "spiritual gifts."

Romans 12:4–8 repeats the same idea in shorter scope. The same trope is used to different effect in Romans 7:4–5. In that context Paul contrasts the old, sinful self ("in the flesh") and the new self "in...the Spirit" or, not surprisingly, "in Christ Jesus" (Rom. 8:1). Here, participation in the body of Christ, the one who died a real, physical death, makes possible the transition from the old to the new self. Paul also knows and uses the eucharistic tradition, that "the bread that we break" is "a sharing in the body of Christ" (1 Cor. 10:16; cf. 11:23–26). Finally, Paul speaks of the "transformation" of human bodies ("the body of our humiliation" or "our humble bodies") into Christ's glorious body (or "the body of his glory") (Phil. 3:21). Clearly, Paul is comfortable with this metaphor as expressive of his understanding of Christ and the church, since he readily turns it to several different uses.

Paul's Metaphorical Language

In addition, Paul frequently uses other metaphors that emphasize physical, bodily reality, particularly those drawn from familial relationships. Indeed, the patriarchal family structure of Paul's day, imagined in its ideal form, exhibited various characteristics Paul wanted to promote among his churches. These include mutual love and care for one another, genuine concern for the well-being of all, a sense that the behavior of any individual reflected on the honor and reputation of the whole group. Above all one might place unquestioned deference to the authority of the father. Typically, Paul's metaphors point to the Divine Father but occasionally set Paul himself in the paternal role. A crucial paradox in Paul's personality and leadership style appears here. Paul considers himself to be absolutely subject to divine authority and conducts himself as a subject of God (in Paul's own words, a "slave of Christ"). He also understands himself to be the divinely appointed messenger who speaks uniquely for God in his particular role ("apostle to the Gentiles"). As such he insists that he should, in this role, be accorded the kind of authority that is elsewhere understood to be reserved for God alone.[5]

Paul enjoys spinning out his favorite metaphors. The familial metaphor takes various twists in his theological reflection. In addition to family love, loyalty, and paternal authority, Paul explores inheritance (Rom. 8:17), adoption (Gal. 4:5–7), childhood and majority (Gal. 4:1–3), betrothal and marriage (2 Cor. 11:2–3), widowhood (Rom. 7:1–3), labor and birthing (Rom. 8:22; Gal. 4:19; 1 Thess. 5:3), nursing and feeding (1 Cor. 3:1–2; 1 Thess. 2:7), and parental instruction (1 Thess. 2:11). Many of these metaphors place a female figure in a role of providence, if not outright authority. We will take up several of these metaphors later in the chapter. Here it will suffice to note that these metaphors may be turned in a direction that reinforces hierarchy, stressing inherent inequality and relationships of control and dependency. They may also be turned in a direction that stresses the intimacy and tender nature of these familial relationships as Paul describes them. This is true even of those that might "formally" be deemed hierarchical.

In addition, we need to ask whether the metaphors that place the congregation in a state of dependence or immaturity (as a child to a parent) should be read as static or dynamic. That is, do we read metaphors of immaturity (say, the nursing infants of 1 Cor. 3:1–2) as describing a persistent state of affairs or aspect of the church's life? Or do we take the metaphor more seriously? We would then argue that infants and children grow up, attain majority, and pass into the roles of authority their parents formerly held. Even so, we as the church today should identify not with the role of dependence that Paul describes for his congregations, but rather with the authority Paul ascribes to himself. Of course, even if we do identify with the parent rather than the child in these familial metaphors, we need to ask whether the paternalistic (or maternalistic) attitude Paul evinces is still an appropriate stance. Nonetheless, the potential for development inherent in these familial metaphors makes it necessary for us to *choose* the moment in which we interpret them.

Paul's Cosmic View and Human Ethics

Our consideration of Paul also needs to take into account his cosmic worldview. Paul frequently theologizes in grand sweeps, encompassing all humankind in his broad generalizations. But Paul's rhetoric does not just catch the human world in his purview. The entire created order often seems to be in view, entrapped in sin or awaiting redemption (see, for example, Rom. 8:22). However we describe Paul's theology, we need to take account of this cosmic scope.

Too often our consideration of Paul's theology seems dissociated from attention to his ethics. One of the signal advances of the "coherence and contingency" way of thinking about Paul's theology is that it takes account of the real world in which Paul functioned and in which his theological principles were constantly being played out. Paul sometimes deals with more intellectual topics at the beginning of his letters and then proceeds to detail how these principles should be lived out in the believing community. Romans offers a good example of this putative division. Still, we should recognize that such a division is artificial for the way Paul thought of the new life in Christ. Whatever being "free from the law" means for Paul, it does *not* mean being free from expectations concerning responsible sexual conduct, respectable behavior, accountability to one another within the congregation, and so forth. Indeed, some of Paul's most difficult struggles (demonstrated particularly in the Corinthian correspondence) seem to be with those who drew the conclusion that Christian theology does *not* have ethical implications.

This ethical emphasis seems to have a pastoral sensitivity close to its heart. In 1 Corinthians 7:10–11, as we have seen, Paul has a word of the Lord (surely a high authority in his religious tradition) regarding divorce. Even so he records an exception, apparently recognizing that not all divorces are the same. Another good example appears in 1 Corinthians 5. A man is living with his stepmother. Paul vigorously denounces both the practice and the congregation's condoning of it. Still, his instructions indicate that the man's punishment is for the purpose that "his spirit may be saved in the day of the Lord" (1 Cor. 5:5). This unwillingness to pronounce a spiritual "death penalty" is clear evidence of Paul's pastoral concern even in the midst of his strong ethical emphasis.

Sociological Implications

We need to understand not only the ethical implications of Paul's theology, but the sociological ones as well. How, exactly, does the coming of Christ change the relationship of Jew and Gentile, such that Peter's decision not to eat with Gentiles in Antioch (Gal. 2:11–14) is not simply a social offense, but out of line with "the truth of the gospel"? Why does Paul seem ultimately dissatisfied with what seems to have been agreed in Jerusalem, one mission for the Jews and another for the Gentiles? Rather, Paul's rhetoric points strongly toward singularity and the abolition of division (a theme carried even further in Colossians and Ephesians). How does Paul expect "being in Christ" to affect the way Jews and Christians interact in the present, physical world? How does the change in relations between Jew and Greek signal changes in the relations of slave and free, and male and female? The place of Galatians 3:28 in Paul's theology is, as we have already seen, an important question to consider. At least, it seems clear from what Paul says at length about Jews and Gentiles that the status "in Christ" has to do with more than the standing of one's soul before God. A change in relationships with other human beings is envisioned. Our exploration of Paul's theology should not neglect this consideration.

Paul's Theology and His Personal Example

In addition, we need to ask how Paul's theology relates to the kind of example Paul understands himself to be to his congregations. Paul clearly shows no reluctance about presenting himself as a model for imitation. Elizabeth Castelli has well termed this call for imitation a "discourse of power." She insightfully notes that by means of the trope of imitation Paul puts himself on a plane with Christ (who is, of course, preeminently to be imitated) and claims for himself unique authority.[6]

While Paul frequently asserts his authority by way of connecting his personal identity with the gospel he proclaims, he often does so via a theme of paradoxical "power…in weakness" (2 Cor. 12:9). The particular rhetorical situation of 2 Corinthians 10—13 may account for the striking frequency of examples of this argument there. It seems quite clear, in this context, that Paul was being compared unfavorably with other evangelists (the "super-apostles," 2 Cor. 11:5; 12:11). He has to turn the accusations leveled against him to his favor by whatever means possible. Still, if as David Clines has argued, Paul is an example of a "man's man,"[7] independent of female aid and disdainful of feminine qualities, it is quite remarkable that Paul ever describes himself as weak, vacillating, dependent on others, distressed—all qualities seen as "womanly" in Paul's world. True, Paul presents these personal qualities to play up the paradox: God is great enough to work even with this. Still, resorting to an argument of paradox demonstrates two important principles: Paul both claims authority and admits that he is an unlikely locus of authority. That paradox has a place in the formulation of Paul's theology. We will need to return to all of these features as we try to discern the best way to understand Paul's theology.

Choosing Where to Look

Finally, we need to consider what is at stake in the quest for a "center" of Paul's theology. I do not necessarily seek to disprove the notion that Paul himself worked out of a core understanding of the gospel. On the other hand, I am not persuaded that scholars can agree on how to approach the core of Paul's theological thought. Nor am I certain that Paul, if he had been asked, would have been able to articulate such a "core." My interest, though, is almost exactly opposite. I want to explore the possibility that the "seams" or inconsistencies in Paul's arguments are clues to the growing edges of his theology. Precisely here we as contemporary interpreters can look for aspects of that theology that point beyond his historical and cultural boundedness. In so doing, I reject the notion that Paul's texts lend themselves to one single correct interpretation. Rather, as we explore these tensions in Paul's thought, we look toward the possibilities they open for us. In so doing we do not deny that these same texts may have opened other possibilities for other interpreters in other times and places. Moreover, in the incoherencies we can see that Paul is pointing beyond that which he is able to articulate in his cultural terms.

Creation and New Creation

In 2 Corinthians 5:17, Paul discusses his task of evangelizing. This text is difficult to translate into English because it is missing some important parts of speech. The text might be rendered:

> Therefore, if anyone [is] in Christ: new creation! The old [things] are gone, behold, new [things] have come about. (Author's translation)

The passage seems to stand at a crucial juncture in Paul's thought. It is preceded by a capsule statement of Paul's gospel:

> one has died for all; therefore all have died. And he died for all, so that those who live might live no longer for themselves, but for him who died and was raised for them. (2 Cor. 5:14b–15)

There follows a discourse on the Christian's calling, described as "the ministry of reconciliation" (v. 18). The phrase "new creation" (*kaine ktisis*) is here linked with Paul's typical designation of the believer, "in Christ." This, it seems, is a way to understand what Paul means by being "in Christ." It is described in terms of the effects of new creation:

1. reconciliation to God, effected by God
2. justification and the nullification of trespasses
3. the involvement of those who are thus newly created in the divine work (v. 19)

As verses 14 and 15 crystallize the proclamation of the gospel, God's saving work in Christ, so verse 19 sums up the effects of being "in Christ." All of this, in turn, revolves around Paul's proclamation: "New creation!" which stands as the linchpin of this text. Here, it seems, is Paul's theology in a nutshell: God's saving act in Christ effects new creation and issues forth in the new life of the believer. The proclamation of "new creation" stands as the single summary of all that happens in the divine act, process, and life of salvation.

But if the idea of "new creation" can be claimed to be foundational to the formulation of Paul's theology, wouldn't we expect him to use the phrase frequently? It only appears in this form (*kaine ktisis*) in one other place in Paul's letters, in Galatians 6:15. Paul spends most of this famously contentious letter arguing against the requirement of circumcision for Gentile believers. Then three verses from the end, he asserts:

oute gar peritome ti estin oute akrobystia alla kaine ktisis.

For neither circumcision is anything, nor uncircumcision, but new creation. (Author's translation)

Paul has not been talking about "new creation" in Galatians. The word *ktisis*, "creation," does not appear elsewhere in the letter. Still, as he summarizes his arguments regarding circumcision, he introduces the phrase. This is, I think, strong evidence that for Paul the notion of "new creation" functions as a central conviction of faith. He does not have to prove this concept. It is not an idea to be argued (as is, say, the non-necessity of circumcision). Rather, it is a grounding conviction, an understanding that frequently "goes without saying," a foundation on which all else is built.[8]

New Creation as Birthing

If, then, "new creation" is a fundamental conviction for Paul, we should be able to see it organizing his thought patterns even when he does not use its specific terminology. Interestingly, one of the passages in which the idea of new creation seems to underlie Paul's argument is a text in which Paul uses metaphorically the female physical experience of birthing. The text is Romans 8:19–23:

> For the creation waits with eager longing for the revealing of the children of God; for the creation was subjected to futility, not of its own will but by the will of the one who subjected it, in hope that the creation itself will be set free from its bondage to decay and will obtain the freedom of the glory of the children of God. We know that the whole creation has been groaning in labor pains until now; and not only the creation, but we ourselves, who have the first fruits of the Spirit, groan inwardly while we wait for adoption, the redemption of our bodies.

We noted this passage in commenting on the cosmic scope of Paul's theological vision. It is important to pay attention as well to what the cosmos is doing: *giving birth*, in the very middle of the birthing process. Paul doesn't directly say what is being born, but presumably the child will resemble the mother. New creation, this metaphor implies, does not simply happen, nor does it happen all at once. It is, rather, brought forth with toil and pain and groaning. Until it has been fully brought forth, it is not possible entirely to say what this child shall be.

The metaphor images positive activity and anticipates positive results. Birthing is, of course, women's work; but it is understood here as productive *work*, not helpless suffering. As Luzia Sutter Rehmann notes, "one who understands giving birth as active work in the service of new life will speak of collaboration in the service of God's new world in a different manner from one who sees giving birth as a passive condition of suffering."[9]

Granted, the text displays a rather clumsy use of metaphor. Creation is awaiting a revelation. Creation is awaiting freedom from bondage. Creation is in labor. "We ourselves" are in labor! What's being born here? Who's doing the pushing? Still, the very clumsiness of the construction may serve as a signal to us that the metaphor is not what's most important in this text. Rather, Paul seeks to express something for which the language of redemption is not quite enough; nor is the language of adoption; nor is the language of freedom from bondage. He adds the metaphor of birth, showing that what is brought into being is entirely new.

To say still more than one metaphor can convey, Paul utilizes this new creation metaphor for all it has to offer. He shows no hesitation in modifying or mixing his metaphors (to the great consternation of literary critics!). Thus, he switches from the cosmic to the personal. Not only is the "whole creation" giving birth, but we "who have the first fruits of the Spirit" are involved as well. Here the birthing metaphor breaks down, so Paul switches to an adoption metaphor without clearly showing how the two are related. Nonetheless, it is clear that, as both the world and humans are subjected to decay, so both the world and humans (specifically, we who are in Christ) are involved in the birthing process for what is to come.

Before we leave the birthing metaphor entirely, though, we need to note how this metaphor also points to other important parts of Paul's theological outlook. In many ways the new creation, the "child," is consistent with its "mother," the old creation. That is, God is the creator of both, and, to add one example, the moral expectations of God's people remain consistent. Paul could describe such expectations as the "fruit of the Spirit" in Galatians 5. This metaphor lets the eschatological horizon of Paul's theologizing appear. He expects the new creation to be completed very soon, although, as many women who have given birth know, the "last few minutes" can stretch out agonizing hours![10]

Paul does not specify what "very soon" means. In 1 Corinthians 7 he advises church members not to marry and start families, and in 1 Thessalonians 4 he apparently does not expect every member of the present generation to die before Christ comes to take "us" away. It is difficult to say exactly where Paul got this understanding of an imminent return of Christ. His thoughts here create something of a problem for us, of course, because he turned out to be wrong in this particular. Still, the eschatological element is quite clearly illustrated in the birthing metaphor, independent of any specific timetable. However long the birthing process may be, it is a process that is absolutely focused on a consummation that is seen to be "soon." Like a successful birth, what exists afterward is utterly and entirely new, a creation that never before existed. I agree with Beker that Paul understands this eschatological existence to be one in which God finally and utterly triumphs. Sin, death, and evil are finally defeated, and the last word belongs to God.[11]

The birthing metaphor does one other thing, though, that I'd like to highlight. It creates for the reader the sense of standing in the middle of a process. Paul very carefully places the present time not in the eschatological time but in the "waiting in eager longing" for it. Another way to say this is that Paul understands his present time as standing *between* creation and new creation. The new creation is not yet fully expressed, not yet quite born. This is not, it should be said, the difference between living in evil and living in good. The original creation is the good gift of a good God, distorted and battered though it is by sin. Still, Paul's metaphor means that all that is promised in the new creation is not yet fully accomplished. Thus Paul can be honest about his own situation, his weakness, his foolishness, his "thorn in the flesh," and so forth, without denying the power of God or the reality of new creation. These, rather, are simply expressions of the first, distorted creation not yet replaced by the reconciled, new creation.

Paul's Use of Scripture

The perspective of new creation also offers us a lens for considering Paul's use of scripture. Here Paul demonstrates his deep loyalty to Israel's sacred texts while reading them creatively, even at times fundamentally altering their apparent meaning for his new situation. It is, in some sense, no surprise that Paul cites scripture. Reared as a Jew and trained as a Pharisee, he undoubtedly would have studied the sacred texts and learned how to exegete them according to the practices of his day. In another sense it *is* noteworthy that Paul cites scripture, and does so regularly. His correspondence is with his *Gentile* churches, made up of people who had not held the Hebrew Scriptures as authoritative tradition. So Paul not only argues *from* scripture, using scripture to support this point or that, but he also argues *for* scripture to persuade his readers that the scriptures of Israel are indeed a part of their heritage, a source of authoritative teaching for them as a faith community in Christ.

Because Paul drank so deeply at the well of scripture, attention to Paul's use of scripture makes us aware of the interpretive possibilities his own writing opens to us. Again, the point is not to prove access to Paul's inner thoughts (although we *may*, in fact, be guessing right) or to claim that Paul is himself some sort of feminist or proto-feminist. Rather, we seek the openings Paul's writings make available to us, the directions in which his texts may reasonably be seen to point, trajectories we can choose to follow.

Given the cumbersome nature of ancient manuscripts and their relative scarcity, individuals were unlikely to own copies of scripture solely for their private use. A copy of the scriptures would be used by the entire community. Teachers like Paul committed large portions of scripture to memory. Paul's readers would understand him to be citing scripture from memory in his letters. Thus it is not surprising that we find variations between Paul's citations of scripture and the written texts (even allowing for the possibility of variants in the manuscripts to which Paul had access). The direction of these alterations, though, provides for us the opening to new interpretive possibilities.

Paul's use of scripture as authority and warrant for his own arguments might lead us to expect him to employ scripture quite conservatively, that is, to choose texts that self-evidently support his point and to cite them explicitly. What we discover in Paul's letters, though, is a use of scripture that is often quite free, creative, and allusive. Occasionally Paul's exegesis changes, even reverses, the original meaning of the text. Thus he reads the

Genesis story of Sarah and Hagar allegorically (Gal. 4:22–31). In so doing he makes Hagar, not Sarah, the mother of "the present Jerusalem" (v. 25). Sarah then becomes the mother of those Gentiles as well as Jews who are "children of the promise, like Isaac" (v. 28). Elsewhere Paul uses scripture to claim that Gentiles are included as part of God's people, as in Romans 2:15, 28–29, where the familiar prophetic metaphor of the "circumcised heart" on which the Law is written (Deut. 10:16; Jer. 4:4; Jer. 31:33) is turned to redefine the people of God.[12] Similarly, Paul unpredictably uses scripture to bolster his claim that the true descendants of Abraham are those who have Abraham's faith, not his physical lineage. Since, according to Genesis, Abraham was reckoned by God as righteous *before* he received circumcision, Abraham can be held up as the faithful progenitor not only of Jews but of "the nations" as well (Gen. 17:5; cf. Rom. 4:13–18).[13] Over and over again, Paul uses the tools of scripture exegesis common in his day to produce readings of the biblical text that likely seemed radical, even novel, to his contemporaries.

These remarkable renderings of scripture cannot be described as evidence of a cavalier attitude toward the sacred texts. On the contrary, Paul understands scripture as conveying the sacred message and participating in that which it conveys. Nor is Paul practicing an exegetical sleight-of-hand, showing off his prowess at making the text mean whatever he wanted it to mean. Rather, Paul's use of scripture is best explained by recalling his location at the nexus of creation and new creation. He is watching the coming-into-being of that which God, who has always been faithful to the present creation, is now creating anew. Both continuity with tradition and the possibility of radical transformation of that tradition characterize Paul's attitude toward and use of scripture.

Adoption and New Creation

One of the ways Paul exegetes scripture creatively for the new creation appears in his development of the metaphor of adoption. We have already touched on Paul's use of familial metaphors. We noted that Paul uses metaphorical language in some surprising ways as well as drawing on some of the stock images found in scripture and in his readers' cultural context. The metaphor of adoption has been one of particular interest to feminist interpreters, as they have grappled with Paul's designation of believers as "sons of God" (*huioi theou*) (Rom. 8:14; 9:26; Gal. 3:26; author's translation). These interpreters have acknowledged that the decision of many modern translations to understand *huioi* inclusively, as applying to all Christians, and thus to translate it "children," obscures the historical realities of adoption and inheritance. To be adopted as a son in Paul's day meant to be granted a share in the inheritance. Adoption as a daughter would not carry the same import. Indeed, the word Paul uses to describe this phenomenon is *huiothesias* (Rom 8:15, 23; Rom 9:4; Gal 4:5; cf. Eph 1:5), built on the *huios* root and perhaps more accurately translated "sonship" than "adoption." Again the structure of Paul's worldview is clear. In that day, all believers, even the females, will receive the privilege of sonship. Once again, it seems, the women will lose their imperfection by being made male. This, apparently, is as good as it gets.

Or is it? In one of his adoption texts (Rom. 8:14–17), Paul begins with "sons of God" (*huioi theou*) (v. 14) and "sonship/adoption" (*huiothesias*) (v. 15). Then, interestingly, he shifts from "sons" (*huioi*) to the grammatically neuter noun "children" (*tekna*) in verses 16 and 17 even though the text goes on to speak of being "heirs" (*kleronomoi*), language that would fit much more naturally with the male "sons" metaphor. Why, then, the switch? This text is also full of language of spirit (*pneuma*), both the human spirit and, most importantly, the Spirit of God. It is easy and, I contend, quite reasonable to imagine that the words of the prophet Joel lie just below the surface of this text. Joel's language reminds writer and readers alike that when the Spirit of God is poured out on all flesh, not only sons but daughters will prophesy (Joel 2:28–32; 3:1–5 LXX). The switch from *huioi* to *tekna* here, then, may be read as a subtle but important reminder that the activity of the Spirit stretches both reality and metaphor.

Sheila E. McGinn builds on Elizabeth Castelli's strategy of feminist discourse analysis for reading Romans—what Castelli calls "using women to think with." McGinn takes the next section of Romans, 8:18–23, as a case study in approaching Romans from a feminist standpoint.[14] We have already considered this text for its birth metaphor. McGinn finds more here than simply a reference to a female physical experience. For McGinn, as for Castelli, the presence of "Spirit" (*pneuma*) in 8:14–17 is less important as an intertextual echo of the gender-egalitarian Joel text than as part of the dualistic construction *kata sarka/kata pneuma* ("according to the flesh"/ "according to the spirit") (Rom. 1:3; 4:1; 8:4–5, 12–13; 9:3, 5). Castelli claims this dualist construction is part of Paul's "ubiquitous" dualistic discourse, a discourse that also favors man over woman, humanity over nature, and so forth.[15] Yet despite what she acknowledges as this duality, McGinn argues that a shift occurs in verses 18–23 that reconfigures the literary context of what has preceded it. Here, she claims, humanity and nature share status as creatures of God:

> We know that the whole creation has been groaning in labor pains until now; and not only the creation, but we ourselves, who have

the first fruits of the Spirit, groan inwardly while we wait for adoption, the redemption of our bodies. (8:22–23)

The result, according to McGinn, is that

this passage…assumes the integration of humanity with nature, and teaches of them both striving together for the same freedom. And it is this freedom of creation, including humanity, which finally reveals the fullness of God's glory. Not only are humanity and nature dependent upon each other and upon God, but even God is dependent on humanity and nature.[16]

McGinn looks at Paul's return to the adoption metaphor. She claims this image should not be read as denying women's gender identity, despite the fact that the image clearly implies adoption "as a son," that is, with full rights of inheritance. On the contrary, she says, to continue to speak of "daughter-heirs" alongside "son-heirs" would imply that the present system of gender inequality is expected to persist into the new order. Rather, the awaited redemption subverts male privilege and reconfigures the relationship, not only of God to humans and humans to nature but also of the genders to one another, so that the eschatological promise includes a vision of equality for all.

McGinn goes on to outline how a Pauline theology of creation, gleaned from this passage, shares many features in common with a feminist theology of creation: a loving Deity, the interconnectedness of all life, the goal of human liberation from structures of domination. Furthermore, she says, Paul goes on to intertwine his creation theology with eschatology, offering a perspective quite different from the violent and destructive eschatological vision from which feminists have often rightly shied away. Paul's eschatology, on the other hand, is "revelation of a reality already nascent in creation's present form. Far from being destroyed, the creation will be liberated to achieve its full potential."[17]

In other words, the emphasis of Paul's eschatological perspective is not consummation, much less holocaust, but new creation. This positive, generative eschatology is another reason, I would argue, to hear in the "Spirit" language of Romans 8:14–17 not so much a dualistic opposition to "flesh" as the echo of the prophet Joel's expectant vision of the last days. The emphasis is on the new that is to come rather than the termination of what currently is, an emphasis well expressed through the laboring-toward-birth metaphor. Of course, the metaphor is not a perfect image of Paul's understanding. For new creation to come into being, it is necessary that the "old has passed away" (2 Cor. 5:17). Yet the emphasis remains on the new that has come and on its vital possibilities for regeneration and liberation.

Fleshing Out New Creation

We can find "new creation" a useful way of getting to Paul's theology in areas other than his eschatology. The eschatological horizon of a new creation, with its emphasis on regeneration rather than annihilation, reflects backward, as it were, into other areas of Paul's theological thought. Stressing the role of God as Creator focuses on the connection between the physical and spiritual order rather than on a putative division or dichotomy of "flesh" and "spirit." Such an emphasis reinforces the physicality of Paul's bodily and familial metaphors. In the new creation we are, and remain, in Christ, members of Christ's body, brothers and sisters of one another. Creation means embodiedness, physicality. This is not a minor point, since Paul came from a worldview that tended to posit a binary division between spirit and flesh and to privilege spirit and its related terms (such as thought, rationality, maleness) over what was related to flesh (body, emotion, femaleness). Living in God's new creation also means that interpersonal and sociological dynamics continue to function, albeit in a transformed way. Ethical standards are upheld and our right relationship to God is mirrored in right, just, and equitable relationships with one another and with the natural world in which we live.

One might, of course, easily object that the trope of "new creation" is rather conveniently vague. Different readers can insert their own expectations of God's goals for the world as they please, and practically anything may be read out of it. The objection is valid. Those who would interpret Paul's theology in terms of "new creation" bear the burden of demonstrating that their readings are plausible and coherent with the general direction of what Paul has to say about God, the world, and human beings. Yet in many ways the very open-endedness of "new creation" recommends it as an appropriate way to approach Paul's theology, since we have already noted that his theology is itself open-ended, in hermeneutical tension between coherence and contingency, difficult to "pin down" on all sorts of particulars. No doubt contemporary interpreters run the risk of construing "new creation" according to their own preconceptions or most deeply held biases. Yet it is also possible to hold the open-endedness of "new creation" as itself a fundamental conviction. Then open-endedness becomes a stance that precludes the ossification of any perspective on the divine work, as God continues to reveal the divine self and to bring into being that which is both new and consistent with the divine nature.

Here we embrace the place of paradox in our theological formulation: Paul's paradox of power in weakness, the paradox of a crucified God, the paradox of holding most firmly to the conviction that God is bringing about change. Here, too, we see that while we may be able to find a theological "center" of Paul's thought, perhaps in the church's historical confession of God's saving act in Christ Jesus, the primary focus is not on the center, but the edges. The theological focus is on those places where we do not yet see what God will do, but where our faith is grounded in the conviction that the Creator is yet at work, making possible reconciliation and new life.

Furthermore, when we see Paul as the *pastor* poised on the brink of new creation, we see a church leader who is extraordinarily aware of the significance of the present moment. Just so, we may posit, he is aware of the present moment for his congregations—the present moment for what each of them is able to receive and integrate into their congregational life. Thus he speaks to that *moment*—not always, as his letters have generally been taken as scripture, as an enduring message for the body of Christ in all times and places. Of course, when we affirm the canon and the church's continuing recognition of these texts as scripture, we point toward an understanding that much of what we have in Paul's letters *is* enduring. These letters *may* be read as having continuing validity. They *do* point toward a gospel that we receive as it was handed down to us. Yet it is patently obvious that in many particulars Paul speaks to his different congregations differently, is concerned with different matters, and takes up a different tone.

Paul's Vision and Today's Church

Clearly much that has happened in the history of the church is strikingly different from anything Paul could have anticipated. For example, Paul seems barely to have imagined that his fellow Jews would not, in relatively short time, come to see things as he did and recognize Jesus as the Christ, God's promised messiah, and the expression of God's plan for the chosen people. Only in Romans 9—11 does Paul consider the possibility that the gospel he has proclaimed so vigorously among Gentiles might not take root in all Jews. There, while still hardly imagining that the state of affairs he knows might persist, he nonetheless affirms that God's gifts and calling to the chosen people are irrevocable (Rom. 11:29).

Christians today who seek to stand in Paul's tradition do so with the knowledge that Judaism has, in fact, continued as a vibrant and flourishing faith tradition. Not only that, but there is also the ugly fact that Paul's texts have been interpreted so as to justify and support suspicion, hatred, discrimination, and slaughter of Jews in the ensuing two millennia. Christian interpreters today, then, have an ethical imperative to seek interpretations of the Pauline texts that acknowledge the continuation of Judaism and repudiate anti-Semitic readings of these texts. Fortunately, scholars of the

Pauline texts today include Christians *and* Jews,[18] as well of persons of other religious traditions or no religious tradition. Members of this community of scholars contribute a great deal to one another, and the Christians who are part of this community particularly are aided in bringing to light the ideological biases in their work. Such dialogue must be nourished and encouraged in order to remain vibrant. As a vigorous and careful debate, it will reveal ways of understanding Paul today that further the well-being of all persons.

Even if we find Paul's eschatological horizon defined as "new creation" more amenable than other eschatological visions, we need to find a way to incorporate this theological perspective into ethical and practical guidance for the church and for the lives of Christian believers today. As we have already noted, Paul's ethic seems, time and time again, to be an interim ethic, appropriate to the moment prior to the inbreaking of new creation. But as an interim ethic, it can also be profoundly conservative, particularly in social terms. Thus it is incumbent on us, as interpreters, to seek to transform Paul's interim ethic into an enduring ethic. We must pick and choose among Paul's directives, particularly those regarding social relationships (gender roles, marriage and singleness, and so on). Indeed, *not* to do so is to refuse to live into the new creation that God is bringing about, even if we still view that new creation as incompletely consummated. Here is the paradox: If we hew too closely to everything Paul tells his correspondents to do, we will have missed the very message of the gospel Paul proclaims, the promise of new creation.

Perhaps part of what we should learn from Paul is how to discern the times: when to confront, when to back off, when to speak authoritatively, and when to encourage others to exercise their own Spirit-led discretion. Paul argues vigorously at times for the surrender of one's own view to the qualms of others as a principle for those who are in Christ (1 Cor. 8:12). At other times he is ready to risk splitting the church rather than give in to such a qualm (Gal. 2:11–12). Neither meat offered to idols nor one's circumcised status are burning issues for most of the church today; yet the decision as to when to acquiesce and when to stand up remains a crucial issue. We can clearly point to instances in which Paul's rhetoric is shaped toward bringing congregations to his point of view. Much has been written about how this rhetoric functions to stifle alternative perspectives, particularly those of women. Still, by assuming that Paul's intent is *always* to force his own perspective, we may be missing those instances (such as his encouragement to eat what is offered with thankfulness and without questioning, 1 Cor. 10:23–31) in which Paul may well be nudging his congregations toward greater openness and toleration. We can see Paul less as enforcing a particular viewpoint than as discerning the appropriate message for the times—albeit times, in Paul's case, that in his judgment required a fair amount of firm guidance. In so doing we may learn from Paul how to discern our times as well and how to preach and lead and minister in the particular circumstances in which we live.

CHAPTER 6

Interpreters of Paul

While the foregoing chapters have treated primarily the biblical texts about which there is wide consensus on Pauline authorship, they do not address all the New Testament books that claim to have been written by Paul. These texts, often called "deutero-Pauline" epistles or "disputed" epistles, are nonetheless important for our consideration because they represent early interpretations of Paul, they have shaped the Christian tradition's perception of Paul, and they may shape our perception of Paul as well. We will approach these texts with some of the same questions and perspectives that have governed our evaluations of the undisputed Pauline texts. We will look for places where women are addressed or referenced and where, in addition, women are "hidden" in the text. We will challenge accepted readings and offer alternatives. Thus we will uncover the ideologies the texts express or incompletely suppress.

Pseudonymity

In the modern industrialized world, we place heavy emphasis on correctly attributing written texts, as well as other types of "intellectual property," to the person or persons who actually wrote or created them. We tend to take a dim view of those who put their names on the work of others (plagiarism) or borrow the name and reputation of another for something they have written (pseudonymity). Even when an author uses a pen name, we expect that name to be an invention, evoking perhaps a certain aura (such as a glamorous-sounding female name for a series of romance novels), but in no case representing the work as the writing of another actual person.

The ancient world saw the situation quite differently. In the absence of printing and mass distribution of written materials, the expectations regarding written texts were rather looser than those of today. A text might be attributed to one of several authors, or the author might be unknown. The text would be judged on its merits rather than its claim of authorship alone. More to the point for our purposes, an author writing in the tradition of another would not be expected to put his (very rarely her) own name to the work. Rather, such an author would ordinarily write pseudonymously, attributing the work to the one who established the tradition.[1] Whether the text was judged authentic or a forgery, then, had less to do with readers' knowledge of its actual authorship than with their evaluation of its faithfulness to the tradition it claimed. If it misrepresented its named author, it was rejected as inauthentic (as indeed were many texts that circulated under the names of biblical figures). But if it was deemed true to the author, it was accepted, whether or not the readers knew with certainty that the named author had actually written the work.

Thus it is not surprising that we have, in the New Testament, several texts that at least some scholars today believe were not written by the authors named in the work. Of these, six are in the Pauline tradition: 2 Thessalonians, Colossians, Ephesians, and the pastoral epistles (1 and 2 Timothy and Titus). Present scholarship reflects varying degrees of agreement on the pseudonymity of these works. Many scholars continue to think that Paul wrote 2 Thessalonians. The scholarly community is divided about evenly on Colossians. More hold for the pseudonymity of Ephesians, while only a fairly small minority argue that the pastoral epistles actually came from Paul's hand (or dictation).[2] Of these, we will leave aside 2 Thessalonians, the least likely to have been pseudonymous and the least important for our particular concerns. The others we will consider in two groups: Colossians and Ephesians together, and then the pastoral epistles.

Colossians and Ephesians: Paul in a New Key

The letters to the Colossians and to the Ephesians[3] are similar, so much so that many scholars think Ephesians is literarily dependent on Colossians (another argument for Ephesians' pseudonymity). In both, the style of writing is more elevated and liturgical than is typical for Paul's other writings (except in his blessings and benedictions). The question of Jew and Gentile seems to have receded from primary focus, and Jesus is presented as the "cosmic Christ," reigning over the universe, and head of his body, the church. (Paul elsewhere uses the metaphor of the church as Christ's body but does not designate Christ as head.) It is, of course, dangerous to argue that any particular writer could not change style, expand metaphors, or adopt new concerns. Still, I find most compelling the notion that both Colossians and Ephesians are not from Paul himself, but a close associate and student of Paul. This anonymous writer would have seen himself as carrying on Paul's tradition most likely (but not necessarily) after Paul's martyrdom. The writer reflects on Paul's theology and builds on his ideas. Thus Ephesians and Colossians should not be used as primary evidence for Paul's theology, but can, I think, be used as important evidence of the way Paul was heard and received by his close cohorts.

In these texts, we see the continued tension between the claims of the gospel and the expectation that believers would continue to function in a highly stratified society. These come to the fore particularly in the "household codes" of Colossians 3:18—4:1 and Ephesians 5:21—6:9. The code in Colossians is fairly straightforward. The Ephesians version is greatly expanded, with theological justification for the exhortations given. The two are similar, however, in many respects, addressing the same members of society in the same order: wives and husbands, children and fathers, slaves and masters.

These codes, about which volumes have been written, are generally approached in one of two basic ways. The first way is to use these texts to demonstrate that Paul's vision does not radically challenge the structures of a hierarchical society or to lament the "demise" of the more egalitarian vision of Paul as a socially conservative worldview triumphs.[4] In this way of reading, these texts, like the Greco-Roman moral literature they parallel, affirm a hierarchical, androcentric social order, with husbands, fathers, and masters in beneficent but firm control of their wives, children, and slaves, respectively. Moreover, the Ephesians text even more explicitly than the Colossians one validates this social order by theological justifications. As we will see, these texts may be read in another way. This way takes account both of the similarities with typical moral literature of the time and notes these texts' characteristic differences.

Colossians 3:18—4:1

Both these texts (we will look first at Colossians) begin as a reader of similar moral literature would expect: an admonition to the subordinate to be subject to the superior, initially to wives regarding husbands, with a theological comment on the appropriateness of such subjection.

> Wives, be subject to your husbands, as is fitting in the Lord. (Col. 3:18)

Then, however, the text takes a turn that would have been unexpected to the first readers: an admonition to the superior, calling him too to responsibility in the relationship:

> Husbands, love your wives and never treat them harshly. (3:19)

While we today may read the directive to the husband and find it disproportionate, what we miss is the rhetorical impact of this unexpected claim that the superior too has theologically justified responsibilities. The text proceeds predictably, commanding children to obey parents, but then again addresses the superiors, this time the fathers, regarding appropriate conduct toward their children.

> Children, obey your parents in everything, for this is your acceptable duty in the Lord. Fathers, do not provoke your children, or they may lose heart. (3:20–21)

The pattern is repeated once more with respect to masters and slaves:

> Slaves, obey your earthly masters in everything, not only while being watched and in order to please them, but wholeheartedly, fearing the Lord. Whatever your task, put yourselves into it, as done for the Lord and not for your masters, since you know that from the Lord you will receive the inheritance as your reward; you serve the Lord Christ. For the wrongdoer will be paid back for whatever wrong has been done, and there is no partiality.
> Masters, treat your slaves justly and fairly, for you know that you also have a Master in heaven. (3:22—4:1)

Slaves are encouraged to equate earthly masters with the heavenly one. The word *kyrios* means "master" or "Lord" and is used in both contexts. Then masters are reminded that they too have a master to whom they owe duty and respect, which they can show precisely by treating their own slaves justly and fairly. The word *isotes* in 4:1, here translated "fairly" (more literally, as a noun, "fairness"), also carries the connotation of "equality."[5] Moreover, each of the subordinates is addressed once (presumably a person is *either* wife *or* child *or* slave), while the male head of household hears his responsibilities triply enumerated. Rhetorically the effect is to stress the differences between the similar moral codes with their typical directives to subordinates only and the mutuality of this Christian social order.

Ephesians 5:21—6:9

The Ephesians version of the household code elaborates on the basic structure. It emphasizes the mutuality implied elsewhere in the code by an opening statement: "Be subject to one another out of reverence for Christ" (Eph. 5:21). The relationship between husband and wife is taken as a metaphor for Christ and the church, with believers' obedience to Christ and Christ's sacrificial love for the church seen as models for the marriage relationship:

> Wives, be subject to your husbands as you are to the Lord. For the husband is the head of the wife just as Christ is the head of the church, the body of which he is the Savior. Just as the church is subject to Christ, so also wives ought to be, in everything, to their husbands.
>
> Husbands, love your wives, just as Christ loved the church and gave himself up for her, in order to make her holy by cleansing her with the washing of water by the word, so as to present the church to himself in splendor, without a spot or wrinkle or anything of the kind—yes, so that she may be holy and without blemish. In the same way, husbands should love their wives as they do their own bodies. He who loves his wife loves himself. For no one ever hates his own body, but he nourishes and tenderly cares for it, just as Christ does for the church, because we are members of his body. "For this reason a man will leave his father and mother and be joined to his wife, and the two will become one flesh." This is a great mystery, and I am applying it to Christ and the church. (5:22–32)

The metaphor, admittedly, becomes strained. It is finally dropped for the direct moral command: "However, each one of you love your wife as yourself, and the wife is to respect her husband" (5:33 author's translation). Both sides of the relationship are theologized, and the emphasis to the wife is on a hierarchical relationship. The greater elaboration, though, is given to the husband's behavior toward the wife and the directive to treat her as he would his own body. Thus the metaphor of head and body, cited to the wife in a manner that suggests traditional hierarchy, is developed in the address to the husband in such a way as to stress the interdependence of "head" and "body."

As Elizabeth Johnson has noted, the image of Israel as God's wife stems from the prophetic tradition (particularly Hosea) and uses marriage to demonstrate divine faithfulness. In Ephesians, however, the direction of the comparison is reversed, making the relationship between Christ and the church the model for human marital relationships. In so doing, the emphasis on faithfulness is subsumed beneath other issues. When the metaphor is assumed to be a description of reality, it becomes open to abuse. Johnson notes, "The comparison of the unity of the church to the unity of a human marriage is yet another image that collapses under the weight of social inequality. Although the religious vision of equality between Jew and Gentile finds concrete expression in the Christian community with the author's blessing, any parallel equality between men and women remains a religious vision rather than a mark of everyday life in the home."[6]

The directive to children is linked to the biblical commandment (Ex. 20:12). Fathers are urged not only not to provoke children, but positively to give them an upbringing in the Lord:

> Children, obey your parents in the Lord, for this is right. "Honor your father and mother"—this is the first commandment with a promise: "so that it may be well with you and you may live long on the earth." And, fathers, do not provoke your children to anger, but bring them up in the discipline and instruction of the Lord. (6:1–4)

Here the word to children implies the father's responsibility as well. If children are to experience the fulfillment of the divine promise of long life and well-being, the fulfillment must result at least in part from the quality of their upbringing "in the discipline and instruction of the Lord." Thus fathers are responsible not only to their children, but also to God, to ensure that the divine promise is indeed fulfilled.

As with the Colossians text, the directive to slaves is lengthy in Ephesians (although not as long as the husband/wife Christ/church metaphor):

> Slaves, obey your earthly masters with fear and trembling, in singleness of heart, as you obey Christ; not only while being watched, and in order to please them, but as slaves of Christ, doing the will of God from the heart. Render service with enthusiasm, as to the Lord and not to men and women, knowing that whatever good we do, we will receive the same again from the Lord, whether we are slaves or free. And, masters, do the same to them. Stop threatening them, for you know that both of you have the same Master in heaven, and with him there is no partiality. (6:5–9)

The comment to masters makes even more explicit the equality of slaves and masters before God, pointing out the divine impartiality. Too, the undercurrent suggesting that Christian slaves do not ultimately belong to their human masters is not far from the surface here.

Reading the Codes

One typical way of approaching the household codes reads the texts for where they *stand,* in a context of clear hierarchy and inequality. Subordinates owe duty to the husband/father/master, and his only responsibility is to treat them with kindness and Christian consideration. The theological metaphors place the superior in a divine role, reinforcing the inequality of the power relation and discouraging challenges to the status quo.

A more promising way of reading these texts, though, reads them for where they *point.* This way follows their *trajectories.* Clearly these texts neither reflect nor prescribe a nonhierarchical society. However, given the context in which they would have first been read, and particularly the rhetorical effect of the "unexpected" directives to superiors, I argue that they point toward a way of understanding society that challenges all hierarchical structures (including the ones these same texts reinscribe). While it is undoubtedly true that the metaphors spun by these texts have elements that reinforce subordination, they may also be read for their emancipative elements, such as mutuality of subjection, the self-emptying of the husband in the description of marriage, and the interdependence of head and body.[7] Truly sacrificial love cannot finally abide hierarchy, as Jesus demonstrates in John's gospel when he washes the disciples' feet and rechristens them "friends" instead of "servants" (Jn. 13:1–17). To treat people with whom one is in a relationship of power truly as children of God every bit as much as oneself requires that one may not use those people for selfish ends. When the household codes are read in this light, they open possibilities of human relationship beyond what could have been imagined in the first century— and toward which we are still challenged to strive.

The Pastoral Epistles: Paul for a New Day

For good reason, more scholars agree on the pseudonymity of the pastoral epistles than on that of Colossians and Ephesians. Characteristic terminology is strikingly different. Jesus is never referred to as "Son" (common in the undisputed letters) but frequently as "Savior" (only at Phil. 3:20 in the undisputed letters). God is often called "Savior" as well. "Godliness" is an important virtue, as is attendance to the "deposit" of faith. While it is true that these letters are presented as private communications to Paul's protégé rather than general instructions to a congregation, and thus deal with different issues (necessitating some different vocabulary), it is unlikely that so much of the theological terminology would change from that used in Paul's letters to churches.

In the pastorals the structure of the church seems to be significantly more complicated than in the undisputed letters. The church has designated offices with specific qualifications for those who hold such offices. The limitation of such designations as "widow" suggests an organization seeking to manage increased demands on limited resources as the church increasingly operates in the public eye. Designations of groups within the church by age and gender point toward issues of religious education, passing the faith on to the next generation. All these would more likely characterize a maturing church than a first-generation one. Thus it seems most likely that the pastoral epistles do not come from Paul himself nor from his own time. Rather, they come from a generation or so later, as the developing church grappled with questions that did not occur, or were not nearly so pressing, in Paul's own time.[8] Moreover, the structures outlined in the pastorals probably represent the author's prescription for what the church should be like, rather than a description of what was happening.[9] Indeed, it is quite likely that the most strongly stressed injunctions signal areas in which the practice of many congregations was *not* what the author of the pastorals thought it should be. His directives counter other leadership patterns and traditions, including some that trace back to Paul.

The amount of attention the pastoral epistles give to the correct conduct of women in the churches signals both the importance of their roles and the controversy that their behavior has created. Women are specifically addressed both as members of the congregation and leaders within it. They are mentioned as particularly susceptible to the incorrect teaching (in the pastoral author's view) that lies at the root of the church conflict.

1 Timothy 2:9–15

The best-known text related to women in the pastorals is likely 1 Timothy 2:9–15, prohibiting women's teaching and enjoining them to silence. The passage is worth citing in full:

> also that the women should dress themselves modestly and decently in suitable clothing, not with their hair braided, or with gold, pearls, or expensive clothes, but with good works, as is proper for women who profess reverence for God. Let a woman learn in silence with full submission. I permit no woman to teach or to have authority over a man; she is to keep silent. For Adam was formed first, then Eve; and Adam was not deceived, but the woman was deceived

and became a transgressor. Yet she will be saved through child-bearing, provided they continue in faith and love and holiness, with modesty.

The passage begins in verse 8 with an injunction for men to pray, and quickly becomes disjointed. Odd transitions make it somewhat difficult to discern precisely what the passage is about other than the conduct and deportment of women in a rather general sense.[10] It is replete with words that connote modesty and discretion. In the first section (vv. 9–10), these qualities are contrasted with the wearing of expensive clothing and jewelry and elaborate hairstyles, suggesting that these are virtues that all the women of the church should emulate, as routinely as they wear clothes or put up their hair.

The passage goes on, however, to address a more strident word toward women who would aspire to leadership. The "I desire" of verse 8 becomes a direct command in verse 11. Both women's learning ("in silence") and their teaching (not to teach men) are addressed. Jouette Bassler points out, however, that the chiastic structure of the passage (*abcb'a'*) makes teaching the central concern. As Bassler notes, the "strictures on speech and authority thus surround and enforce the central prohibition: If a woman is not permitted to speak or exercise authority, she surely will be unable to teach."[11]

The injunction is bolstered by a theological warrant that relies on an order of creation (Adam came first) and order of fall (Eve sinned first). The hierarchy it constructs recalls 1 Corinthians 11:7–9, although this text is less convoluted than the Corinthians passage. First Timothy 2 is markedly out of step with Paul's more extensive theological reflection on the Fall in Romans 5:12–21, where *Adam's* disobedience leads to sin's reign in the world.

Perhaps the oddest part of this passage, though, is verse 15. This verse seems to establish a requirement for women's salvation—namely, childbearing—that is nowhere else supported in scripture. The grammar and syntax of this verse are difficult enough, notably a shift in subject from singular to plural halfway through the verse.[12] Some have suggested that the "they" at the end of the verse refers to the woman's children. The additional theological difficulties entailed by the notion that a woman's salvation depends on her children's conduct are problematic enough to lead most interpreters to reject this interpretation. Thus we go back to the understanding that the "she" of the first part of the verse and the "they" of the latter part both have "woman" (in the general sense) or "women" as referent.

But could the author of the pastorals possibly be claiming that motherhood is prerequisite for salvation? The heterodoxy of such an assertion compels a search for other interpretations. One attractive possibility is to suggest that "be saved through" (*sothesetai dia*) childbearing here should be read in a physical, rather than soteriological, sense. As we have noted, childbearing was the greatest danger to the life of a woman once she survived to adulthood and thus an event many women deeply feared. In this sense, being "saved through childbearing" would mean preservation during the most difficult times of a woman's life and by extension a promise of God's abiding presence. This interpretation faces one major drawback. The verb *sozo*, "to save," would here be interpreted in a sense different from that which it commonly carries in the pastoral epistles (1 Tim. 1:15, "Christ Jesus came into the world *to save* sinners"; see also 1 Tim. 2:4; 4:16; 2 Tim. 1:9; 4:18; Titus 3:5). Nonetheless the word is commonly used, in the New Testament and elsewhere, to mean preservation from natural dangers and afflictions. Such a reading here both avoids the theological difficulty of claiming salvific efficacy for childbearing and offers a sense that would have been meaningful and reassuring to the text's first female hearers.

Another possibility is to read *teknogonias* not as "childbearing" or "childbirth," in the general sense, but rather as "birth of the Child," that is, Jesus. It is a lovely poetic turn—"she (who bears children) will be saved through the birth of the Child"—but it is somewhat difficult to accept this reading in a text that is generally quite wooden and *not* given to poetic nuance.

It remains impossible to rule out a view with deep theological problems. The author of the pastorals apparently combats ascetic teachings. One way to do this is to insist that women follow a non-celibate path to salvation. This path, if not *requiring* childbearing, then at least prescribes that women pursue salvation through acceptance of the traditional domestic gender role.

Titus 2:2–10

Elsewhere, the pastorals likewise seek to circumscribe women's roles and activities, both in leadership and as members of the congregation. In Titus 2:2–10, rules of behavior are laid out that presumably encompass every member of the congregation: older and younger men, older and younger women, and slaves. The instructions to older women, in verses 3–5, include the directive that the older women should teach the younger (the younger women are not instructed directly in the passage). The content of this teaching is spelled out in detail. Presumably the older women are expected to be models of behavior, as well as instructors. They are to train their younger sisters "to love their husbands, to love their children, to be self-controlled, chaste, good managers of the household, kind, being submissive to their husbands, so that the word of God may not be discredited" (vv. 4b–5). In addition, the older women are instructed to be reverent, not slanderers, or "enslaved to much wine" (v. 3, author's translation). Interestingly, in this passage only the older women and the letter's addressee ("Titus") are given tasks. Titus is to set an example, and the older women are to teach the younger. Part of the reason for this may have been the social conventions of a gender-segregated society, in which girls and young women received the bulk of their education from older female relatives. It is also quite possible, however, that this directive aimed to rechannel an activity currently going on. Older women were teaching, and it was fruitless to attempt to keep them from teaching. The writer decided it was more productive to channel their teaching into "proper," carefully defined and delimited situations and topics.

1 Timothy 3:11

Two texts in 1 Timothy specifically address the conduct of women in leadership roles. Scholars have long debated whether *gynaikas* in 1 Timothy 3:11 should be read as "wives" (that is, the wives of deacons) or "women" (who have a leadership role similar to that of the male deacons). Either is possible with the Greek word, and neither makes complete sense in context. If "wives" is meant, the phrase seems incomplete without a possessive pronoun ("*their* wives"). If "women" is intended, one would expect to see the name of their office parallel to "bishop" and "deacons" in the same passage. In any case, given that the expectations for the behavior of a deacon extended to his family (v. 12), these women function as leaders in the congregation, whether as a part of the deacons' model families or as functionaries ("deaconesses"?) in their own right. Such women, the pastoral author says, should "be serious, not slanderers, but temperate, faithful in all things." Again, special attention is given to these women's speech as well as their qualities of temperance and faithfulness, presumably, to the pastoral author's patriarchically structured model of the gospel.

1 Timothy 5:3–16

More extensive attention is given in 1 Timothy 5:3–16 to a group of women referred to as "widows."

> Honor widows who are really widows. If a widow has children or grandchildren, they should first learn their religious duty to their own family and make some repayment to their parents; for this is pleasing in God's sight. The real widow, left alone, has set her hope on God and continues in supplications and prayers night and day; but the widow who lives for pleasure is dead even while she lives. Give these commands as well, so that they may be above reproach. And whoever does not provide for relatives, and especially for family members, has denied the faith and is worse than an unbeliever.

Let a widow be put on the list if she is not less than sixty years old and has been married only once; she must be well attested for her good works, as one who has brought up children, shown hospitality, washed the saints' feet, helped the afflicted, and devoted herself to doing good in every way. But refuse to put younger widows on the list; for when their sensual desires alienate them from Christ, they want to marry, and so they incur condemnation for having violated their first pledge. Besides that, they learn to be idle, gadding about from house to house; and they are not merely idle, but also gossips and busybodies, saying what they should not say. So I would have younger widows marry, bear children, and manage their households, so as to give the adversary no occasion to revile us. For some have already turned away to follow Satan. If any believing woman has relatives who are really widows, let her assist them; let the church not be burdened, so that it can assist those who are real widows. (1 Tim. 5:3–16)

At first glance the primary concern seems to be an economic one. This passage affords us a valuable window into the social ministry of the early church. Without governmental assistance, people unconnected to a source of income (widows, orphans, people unable to work) were dependent on family or private charity to avoid abuse or destitution. The church apparently provided particularly for widows. This practice could easily come to entail considerable expense, as this passage indicates by rules designed to limit the number of applicants. A woman to be supported by the church should be at least sixty years of age (and thus an unlikely candidate for remarriage), without the possibility of support from children or extended family, and with a history of good works and Christian behavior. These rules appear to have served the economic purpose of identifying the most needy while limiting the burden on the church by keeping women from joining the community for the sole purpose of receiving its economic assistance.

On closer inspection, however, more seems to be involved in the treatment of "widows" than purely economic issues. The "real widow" of 5:5 is involved in ministry activities ("supplications and prayers"). Many of the qualifications in 5:10 for enrolling a widow ("shown hospitality, washed the saints' feet, helped the afflicted, and devoted herself to doing good in every way") are a laundry list of the Christian behaviors elsewhere expected of church leadership. The requirements beyond simple economic need suggests that women recognized as "widows" by the church are expected to perform certain duties (and thus must be above reproach in their personal lives, as is also true for the "bishop" of 3:1–7 and the "deacons" of 3:8–13).

Most telling, though, is the author's seemingly harsh treatment of "younger widows" in 5:11–15. He claims they will violate "their first pledge" if they choose to marry. Since marriage, and not remarriage, is spoken of here, it is likely that not only women bereaved at a young age, but also women who wished to forego marriage and family altogether, were petitioning to be accepted as part of the church's "widows." As such they would enter a pledge that would involve a life of prayer and supplication as well as celibacy. As we have already seen, the author of the pastorals deeply mistrusts the celibate life, connecting it inextricably with his theological opponents' teaching. Thus we are not surprised that here, once again, he presumes the worst of those who would choose celibacy when marriage and childrearing are an option. The writer assumes first that they will find sexuality so alluring that they will break their oath. Then they will disrupt other households, perhaps even teaching the opponents' scandalous message. Once again, the pastoral author's distrust of celibacy becomes the controlling factor. He cannot abandon the church's tradition, rooted in longstanding Jewish tradition, of special care for widows, so he downplays what was likely their important role in the church. In addition, he seeks to keep their numbers, and thus their influence, as small as possible, and to limit their ranks to those who had already demonstrated their allegiance to life in the patriarchal household.[13]

1 Timothy 4:7; 2 Timothy 3:6–7

Finally, we see the pastoral author seeking to discredit his opponents' message by associating that message with women. First Timothy 4:7 calls on Timothy to reject "profane and old-womanly myths" (author's translation), contrasting these with "words of the faith" and "sound teaching" (v. 6). Second Timothy 3:6–7 describes the false teachers of the last days as those who "make their way into households and captivate silly women, overwhelmed by their sins and swayed by all kinds of desires, who are always being instructed and can never arrive at a knowledge of the truth." Verses 2–5 have already characterized these teachers in an exceptionally long list of vices. The Greek word translated "silly women" is *gynaikaria*, a diminutive of *gyne*, "woman." The word choice vividly illustrates the author's lack of respect for the women in question. By caricaturing both them and the opponents with the same broad stroke, the pastoral author demonstrates his distrust of the community's women and betrays his prejudice against them.

Conflict and Hierarchy

The author of the pastoral epistles takes the Pauline tradition in a particular direction. The church situation is one of conflict. The author makes veiled references to other teachers, whose instruction he characterizes as false, dangerous, or heretical. Because the author assumes Paul's persona and specifies Timothy, who was receiving this particular teaching, as his true and legitimate heir, we may also be confident that the conflict is, at least in part, over the ownership and transmission of the Pauline tradition. Seeking further certainty than this about the views and purposes of the various parties in the conflict is difficult. The difficulty rises from the fictional structure required by pseudonymity and from the rhetorical technique that borrows content as well as conventions from the prevailing culture.

Nevertheless it seems reasonable to posit some elements of the false teachings the author of the pastorals combats. This interpretation of Paul's teaching apparently rejects the goodness of the created order, repudiates marriage and family life, and restricts God's saving activity only to those with a special knowledge. The author of the pastorals sees his opponents as teaching all or some combination of these. In contrast, the Pastoral author emphasizes God as the savior of all (1 Tim. 2:4, 6; 4:10; 6:13; Titus 2:11) and creation as God's good work (1 Tim. 4:4). He strongly affirms familial relationships among the people of God in the metaphor of the divine household (1 Tim. 3:15).

In developing these emphases, however, the author of the pastorals traces Paul's trajectories in the direction of the familial and social structures he knew: the hierarchical, patriarchal structures of the Greco-Roman world. The model of "household" that held sway in the Roman Empire becomes the author's model for the divine household. While such a model had a place for everyone in it—young and old, married and single, male and female, slave and free—it also represented a system that rigidly kept everyone in his or her place. From our very different vantage point, we easily recognize the weaknesses of this model when it is taken as the paradigmatic interpretation of Paul, applicable beyond the specific crises of the pastoral author's situation. More instructive, and more difficult to discern, is the way the pastoral epistles can function for us as both a directive and a warning in the tracing of Pauline trajectories and in claiming universal application for the directions we trace.

The Acts of Paul and Thecla: Another Side of Pauline Tradition

While Colossians, Ephesians, and the pastoral epistles represent Pauline traditions that received the endorsement of the church through canonization, other Pauline traditions existed from early on and received widespread acclaim. The best-known and best-understood of these is represented by the text known as *The Acts of Paul and Thecla*, a document that seems to have circulated shortly after 150 C.E. and was based on narratives circulated much earlier. Indeed, the warnings in the pastoral epistles against "old wives' tales" (1 Tim. 4:7) are taken by some scholars to be references to the Thecla and similar traditions.[14]

The Thecla narrative is part of a larger set of narratives known as the *Acts of Paul*, in which Paul preaches asceticism and sexual renunciation and is involved in various escapades.[15] The story begins with Thecla, a young woman of Iconium, who is betrothed to a man named Thamyris. Hearing Paul's preaching at the house of Onesiphorus, she becomes captivated by his discourse on virginity. Persuaded by Paul's teachings, she breaks her engagement to Thamyris. When Thamyris has Paul imprisoned, she goes to him in prison to hear more of his teaching, bribing the gatekeeper with her bracelets. Paul is cast out of the city. Thecla is condemned to be burned, but a divinely appointed storm puts out the fire and endangers many of the onlookers with flood and hail. Paul proceeds from city to city. Thecla follows him, inciting both admiration and opposition. Frequently in danger of her life, she always escapes death by miraculous means. Along the way she baptizes herself and continues to teach and proclaim the word of God. When she is finally reunited with Paul, he first suspects her intentions. She reassures him she serves the same God as he, and he finally sends her forth to teach the word of God.

The *Acts of Paul and Thecla*, as it now appears, seems clearly to be embroidered with legend. When Thecla is thrown to the wild beasts, a fierce lioness comes to her defense and kills all the other lions and bears sent to destroy her. When she dives into a pit of water to baptize herself, the flesh-eating seals in the pit see a flash of lightning and float dead on the surface of the water. Despite these legendary accretions, though, the core of *Paul and Thecla* seems quite clearly to be a different tradition concerning Paul. Not only does this Paul expect asceticism and sexual abstinence of those who seek God, but he also explicitly, if somewhat reluctantly, affirms the ministry of a woman who follows his teachings. The persistence of these traditions, albeit outside the canon, is evidence that some of those who understood themselves to stand in the Pauline tradition read Paul very differently than the tradition of the pastorals. Feminist readers today may reject the model of an ascetic virgin for the ideal woman in ministry. In ancient times, however, sexuality was so inextricably intertwined with a hierarchical social order that a woman's freedom to travel and proclaim would logically have been connected with the repudiation of marriage and family life.

Paul in Early Church Interpretation

The interpretation of Paul in the early church offers instructive examples of the ways patristic authors followed various Pauline trajectories in directions that addressed the perceived needs of the various audiences to which they wrote. A good case study can be found in the interpretation of 1 Corinthians 7. As church historian Elizabeth Clark has demonstrated, nearly all these authors valued sexual abstinence more highly than marriage, though they opposed the heretical asceticism of the Manichees and the Marcionites. Still, "orthodox" patristic writers interpreted the injunctions of 1 Corinthians 7 differently. As Clark says, "words designed to chastise overly ascetic Marcionites were ineffective in rousing self-indulgent married Catholics to sexual restraint."[16] Moreover, since these writers took the pastorals, Colossians, and Ephesians as authentically Pauline as the other letters, they faced the challenge of interpreting a "Paul" who spoke quite differently in different texts regarding marriage and remarriage, procreation, and sexual renunciation. 1 Corinthians 7, Clark notes, was rarely interpreted in the eschatological context stressed by modern commentators.[17] Rather, they interpreted Paul's tone and supposed audience to determine whether his various directives were words of concession to those who were too weak to practice renunciation or encouragement to the higher calling of the celibate life.

"Commands" and "Counsels"

Clark proceeds to look at each passage in 1 Corinthians 7. She demonstrates how various patristic writers—all of whom valued chastity more highly than marriage, but disagreed on the value of marriage—make sense of these texts.[18] They all take Paul seriously. Indeed, they understand him to be divinely inspired, so that one of their points of discussion is the places (verses 6, 10, 12, 25) where Paul indicates that he has a "command of the Lord" compared to those where he appears to speak on his own authority. Should Paul's own advice not be taken as seriously as the words Paul indicates came by divine command? After all, Paul himself comments at the end of the chapter that he has "the Spirit of God" (v. 40). Still, these distinctions must mean *something*.

Although they draw out the implications in somewhat different ways, the patristic writers tend to agree that in this chapter Paul states both "commands" required of all Christians and "counsels" for those who wished to strive for perfection (and, ultimately, for a greater heavenly reward). Thus the patristic authors understand Paul to presuppose a fundamental distinction in the church. This distinction would take shape in the patristic period between the religious orders and the laity. Barring an imminent eschatological horizon, they read Paul's appraisal of virginity as "better" than marriage as a perpetual verdict set out in the first verse of the chapter and frequently reinforced thereafter.

The patristic writers found it impossible to agree on the tone with which Paul's comments on sexuality should be understood. As is the case with many interpreters today, some patristic writers took Paul's comments on married sexuality as qualified commendation, while others read them negatively as the narrowest concession, necessary only to avoid greater evil. Particularly problematic is the statement in verse 1 (taken to be Paul's own view): "It is good for a man not to touch a woman" (NASB). "Good" compared to what? Tertullian and Jerome, for example, argue that the opposite of a virtue is always a vice. Thus if "not touching" is "good," then "touching" is necessarily always tainted.[19] Augustine, on the other hand, claims that a good can only be compared with another good. Comparing a "good" with an evil would make it good only in relation to that greater evil, and thus both would be evils. Paul can compare virginity and marriage, according to Augustine, only because he understands both to be "good."[20] Contributing to the difficulty of judging whether "touching" (generally understood as sexual contact) could be considered "good" is the description in verse 5 of the married couple who are temporarily abstinent to devote themselves to prayer. For more ascetically minded authors, this is additional evidence that sexual incontinence, even within marriage, is detrimental, since it is not compatible with prayer.

The patristic writers also debate the meaning of verse 34, which states that unmarried women and virgins "are anxious about the affairs of the Lord, so that they may be holy in body and spirit." Does this mean, then, that the married woman, sexually active, bearing children, and keeping a household, is not capable of holiness? Some authors use this argument to counsel young women against marriage; Augustine claims, though, that it is possible for a married woman to be "holy in body and spirit" by being subject to her husband, as is described in Ephesians.[21]

Origen notes that, in verse 28, Paul describes marriage as "not a sin." Origen contrasts this appraisal with the "good" reserved for abstinence. Still, the majority of patristic authors take Paul seriously here. They even use him in their debates against the even-more-ascetic Montanists. These early church fathers are willing to permit marriage between those not already pledged to chastity. After all, they reason, it does guard against fornication. Tertullian reasons further, if God permits marriage as a remedy, then extramarital sex must be unforgivable sin.[22]

The Troubles of Marriage

While some authors threaten sexual sinners with hellfire, many others urge chastity by detailing the woes of married life here and now. Jerome understands the "impending distress" of verse 26 to be "swelling wombs and wailing infants."[23] John Chrysostom's enumeration of the woes of the married state is worth quoting at some length:

> Courting time is at hand. One anxious thought after another, various in nature, comes to mind immediately: what husband will the girl get? Will he not be low-born, dishonorable, arrogant, deceitful, boastful, rash, jealous, penurious, stupid, wicked, hardhearted, effeminate? Of course, all of this need not be true for every bride, but it must be anxiously pondered by them all...When the wedding day arrives, the woman's anguish intensifies. Her pleasure diminishes as her fear grows that from that very evening any disagreeable trait will appear in her and she will fall far below his expectation. It is bearable to be held in esteem at the beginning and later to be despised. However, if she appears insipid from the starting-line, so to speak, when in the future can she be the object of his admiration?...Yet, once that anxiety is eased, the fear of childlessness straightway replaces it. In addition, there is the conflicting worry of too many children. Since the future is unknown, she is disturbed by both these fears from the beginning. If she becomes pregnant immediately, once again joy is mixed with fear—nothing that has to do with marriage is without fear. She fears that she might lose in a miscarriage what has been conceived and being pregnant her own life will be endangered. If, on the other hand, the pregnancy is protracted, the wife does not speak freely, as if she were in charge of the hour of delivery. When the time of birth is at hand, labor pains rend and tear the hard-pressed womb for an incredible time; such pain is sufficient by itself to overshadow the good aspects of marriage. Other cares along with these trouble her. The poor miserable girl, although so tormented in this way by pain, fears no less than it that a damaged and crippled baby be born instead of one perfect and healthy, that it be a girl and not a boy...When the child is born and gives its first cry, concern for its safety and upbringing succeeds in turn her earlier cares. Even if the child is naturally inclined and adapted for virtue, again the parents fear that their offspring will suffer something terrible, or that he will die prematurely, or that he will change into something wicked; for good children grow into mean and wicked

men, as well as wicked children do into honest men. And if one of these dreadful possibilities arises, it is more intolerable and painful for the woman than if it had happened initially…However, all married couples do not have children. Do you acknowledge in its turn another reason for despondency? So, whether they have children or not, who are either good or bad, parents are afflicted by diverse and distressing cares…But again, if a couple lives in harmony, their fear is that death will burst in and end their pleasure. Rather, there is no longer only this fear and the expectation of it; there is also the knowledge that they must inevitably, without a doubt, advance towards death…What should we say of the separations that take place in the meantime, the long absences abroad, the anguish accompanying them, the illnesses?…But let all this be passed over and let us in no way accuse the institution of marriage. Yet we will be unable to extricate it from the following charge. What sort of charge is it? That marriage does not allow someone of sound health to be better off than a sick man but reduces him to the same state.[24]

Only a virgin, insist the patristic authors, can be truly free. A married woman is in servitude to her husband, they point out, recalling Genesis 3:16. Thus she cannot also serve God. In fact, commentators such as Origen and Jerome take Paul's comments about "slavery" and "freedom" in verses 17–24 not as digression, but as a continuing, albeit metaphorical, discussion of the marital state. Obligation to sexual intercourse is "slavery." One can become "free" even within marriage by agreeing to continence and by practicing virtue. The greater "freedom" is, of course, experienced by the unmarried person who is thus a "slave of Christ."[25] Interestingly, Augustine does not seem to follow this reading of this passage. He objects to those who emphasize marital woes as a way to urge persons toward celibacy. His reasons are exegetical and theological. Paul wrote, he argues, to bring individuals to eternal life, not to protect them against domestic worries. The interpreter and preacher should have similar motives.[26]

Making Paul Fit

In developing these readings, the patristic authors expand some emphases in 1 Corinthians 7 and qualify or circumscribe others. The sexual mutuality in verse 4 draws their attention. Chrysostom, for one, warns that the equality implied here does not extend to other areas of a couple's life.[27] These authors discuss how a wife might "save" her non-Christian husband (v. 16) if, as 1 Timothy 2:12 says, women are not permitted to teach. Some resolve the problem by deciding that 1 Timothy refers to public teaching and that private instruction at home would be allowable. Chrysostom, again, has a thoughtful interpretation. Noting that women are barred from teaching because of Eve's role in the introduction of sin, he reasons that, if men become the sinful gender, they may be saved by virtuous women.[28] Paul's comparatively lax attitude toward divorce also troubles many of the patristic interpreters. Some try to qualify Paul's teaching to bring it in line with the instructions of Jesus, often noting that Paul speaks specifically of mixed marriages, while Jesus instructed Christian couples. Augustine notes that Paul permitted divorce if the unbelieving partner insisted (v. 15), while Jesus permitted divorce only on grounds of adultery. From this he concludes that paganism is, in fact, a form of fornication, so that a believer who is divorced by his or her non-Christian spouse has not fallen foul of Jesus' command. Others found Paul's and Jesus' teachings more difficult to reconcile, and, like Origen, distinguish here between Paul's authoritative teaching and the still more authoritative law of the Lord.[29]

Probably the most difficult part of the chapter for these authors' readings, though, is 7:7, with its clear implication that both marriage and celibacy are gifts from God. Some, interestingly, accept this idea at face value. Concord, says Origen, is the special gift of marriage, as holiness is the special gift of celibacy. Each gift can only be received by Christians. Ascetics retort: but even pagans apparently experience concord in marriage, so it must not be a divine gift. Calling virginity a "gift" also proves problematic, as it suggests that some believers would receive it without striving for it, while for others any attempt would be in vain.[30] The debates so joined quickly escalate to discussions of grace versus free will and the question of whether something received as a gift can garner heavenly reward—reward which, as we have seen, the patristic authors are certain attaches to the practice of earthly continence.

Conclusions from the Church Fathers

While investigation of the interpretation of a single Pauline chapter obviously does not unfold all the ways authors of the patristic period understood and explained Paul, it does offer certain insights. First, it demonstrates that the interpretation of Paul in Christian tradition has never been univocal. Different interpreters hear Paul's tone differently. They stress some passages in the text while downplaying others. Where Paul appears vague, they "fill in the blanks" differently. They use different philosophical approaches to determine what is being censured by a positive command or encouraged by a prohibition. Such study in patristics also illustrates the influence of social and theological location on interpretation. None of these authors would have allowed that Paul's words could mean "anything the interpreter wants them to mean." Indeed, they regarded Paul as divinely inspired authority and held every verse in high esteem. Nonetheless, their foundational conviction regarding the superiority of celibacy to marriage favors certain readings and makes others impossible. Finally, our study here shows that the interpretations that did hold sway in the early church tended toward prescribing a narrow selection of roles for women. A woman could be holy and pure, even, according to some authors, throwing off her femaleness altogether if she chose to dedicate herself to God and live according to the church's expectations of virgins. Or, if she married and participated in family life, she should do so as befits a Christian woman: submissive to her husband, fulfilling the roles of wife and mother above all else. Other options were outside the bounds or were simply not considered.

Paul in Feminist Perspective

A full review of the history of Pauline interpretation is beyond the scope of this volume. Paul's stated preference for celibacy for those who serve God (1 Cor. 7:32–35) continued to undergird the Roman Catholic social structure. Worship leadership was limited to unmarried males; women were generally permitted to live dedicated lives only under circumscribed conditions. Meanwhile, Martin Luther famously found in Paul a kindred spirit for his anxiety over a rule-bound religious practice. In turn, the Lutheran view of Paul largely reigned in Protestant interpretation until the past few decades. The movement away from the "Lutheran Paul" has focused largely on Paul's view of the Law and his understanding of Judaism, but often has not had much to say about Paul's position on the role of women.[31]

For centuries, women interpreters of scripture often had little to do with Paul except, it seems, to point out that their experience of God and of the divine claim on their lives seemed not to square with Paul's expectations of the feminine gender. As we have noted (chap. 2), early feminist interpreters of the New Testament tended to focus on the figure of Jesus, his remarkably open relationships with women disciples and interlocutors, and thus his unique place in his "Jewish environment." Paul's attitude toward women, when it received attention at all, was often overtly or subtly attributed to his "Jewish past," incompletely converted by his encounter with Jesus and uninfluenced by Jesus' egalitarian teachings.

Such a picture of the first-century situation does injustice, of course, to the nature of pre-70 (as well as later) Judaism, which has emerged in recent research as a vibrant and multifaceted phenomenon in which women's roles were far from predictable.[32] Similarly, it is extraordinarily difficult to trace the cultural patterns of influence on Paul, a diaspora Jew apparently educated in Greek thought and thoroughly at home in the urban centers of the eastern Roman Empire. Nonetheless, Paul's seemingly clear words of limitation on women, whatever their root, have led many feminists to concur with the oft-quoted evaluation of George Bernard Shaw that Paul is "the eternal enemy of woman."

Thus many women, particularly those who have sought roles of church leadership, tend to view Paul as the instrument with which they are bashed. Still, feminist readers (both female and male) have long noted that not all Paul's comments on women are in the same vein. The past several years have seen a proliferation of articles, monographs, and collections that address the hermeneutical questions raised by Paul's letters and particularly his comments on women, with an eye to discerning a meaningful word for women in the church today. Many of these works are listed in the Bibliography of the present volume. Others are just being published, or will emerge in the next few years. Suffice it to say that this significant literary output demonstrates that feminist biblical scholars, critics, and theologians are not done with Paul. Rather, there remains much to say, and much to ponder, and this book is a contribution to that continuing undertaking.

CONCLUSION

―――――――

Reading Paul Today

The reader of Paul's letters today brings various presuppositions and expectations to the text. Indeed, many readers of Paul, or citers of Paul's words, are not members of traditional Christian communities. The household codes of Colossians and Ephesians, taken to be Paul's, reinforce conservative political stances of appropriate gender and family relations that go far beyond theologically grounded arguments. Sentiments lifted from 1 Corinthians 13 show up in the weddings of people who have never read Paul's letters and do not know the words' original context, except perhaps that they are "from the Bible." A reader so unlikely as the secular Marxist theorist Alain Badiou has recently championed Paul as a radical revolutionary thinker, refusing to accept the world as it is and proclaiming new ideals with a view to bringing about a more just world order.[1]

The Nature of Biblical Authority

For theologically committed Christian readers, though, Paul's words are more than data for historical study or philosophical contemplation. We stand in a relationship with these texts. The language of "authority" has often been used to describe this relationship. For many readers this relationship has been oppressive or abusive, and for some interpreters "authority" is no longer an appropriate term. In a perceptive article titled "A New Teaching with Authority," Mary Ann Tolbert considers the "special hermeneutics" (a term drawn from Rudolf Bultmann) with which the Bible has been interpreted. She suggests that rather than speaking of the Bible as "authoritative," we should consider another view of the Bible in the church, that of the Bible as "inspirational" in the fullest sense:

> Scripture is able to inspire, literally to "breathe in," the hope, religious joy, and vision of its ancient authors and audiences. It does not dictate what our current views, hopes, or visions should be but instead allows us to witness the successes and failures of those before us in the struggle to be faithful doers of the will of God. Their courage in their particular historical contexts can inspire us to be courageous in our own historical situations. But their social, cultural, and theological limitations need not be adopted in the present world as God's eternal command, as they now often are. Understanding the Bible as the inspirational, rather than authoritative, center of Christian fellowship requires contemporary Christians, much like the earliest Christians, to take full responsibility for their own theological and ethical decisions. Interpretations of the Bible can no longer be used as a warrant or proof-text to disguise the human drives to power and control of its readers. Like Paul and the Corinthians, modern Christians will have to define and argue for their own theological positions in open encounter with those whose theological positions are quite different, without hiding behind the Bible as guarantee that one is right and the other is wrong.[2]

Seeing the Bible as inspiration rather than authority, Tolbert argues, makes it possible for us to revitalize our readings of the text. It lets us involve both clergy and (especially) laity in considering how the Bible may be read to encourage us toward a vision of a just and diverse global society. It still leaves us free to reject the ways these same texts have been used to demean, marginalize, and exclude.[3]

I do not agree with Tolbert's suggestion that "inspiration" and "authority" be cast as opposing terms. Rather, I see "inspiration," in the full sense that Tolbert describes, as one way of understanding the texts' authority. Much of what she says about an "inspirational" understanding of scripture, however, fits well with what I have called a "transformational" reading. Tolbert's distinctions remind us that we must not simply choose bits of the text (say, what we find liberating) and accord those pieces the same sort of authority that was previously claimed for more oppressive parts of the text.

Rather, the notion of authority is itself transformed. This kind of authority, in Tolbert's words, "does not dictate what our current views, hopes, or visions should be." Instead, it empowers us to pursue lines of thinking further than the text itself, in its historical and cultural boundedness, goes. Remembering that interpretation of the text has never been univocal, we read the texts closely to find their seams and tensions. Then we dig in precisely at these points, calling the text to witness against itself and taking responsibility for the interpretations that we derive from it.

A Pauline Theology of New Creation

Redefining authority in this way abandons the comfortable certainty of proof-texting. Attempting a transformational reading of the Pauline texts is a bold move. But as the foregoing chapters have demonstrated, Paul's letters support a reading centered on *new creation* as the place where Paul's ideas open toward genuine possibilities for a feminist perspective. New creation articulates the conviction that God has done something radically new in the Christ-event. This new way of being not only concerns the individual's relationship with God but also includes the relationships of human beings with one another. Indeed, it encompasses all of the created order. Spinning out the continuing ethical, sociological, and pastoral implications of new creation is one of the central tasks of the church.

Standing at the moment of birth of the new creation, we affirm our connection with tradition while staying open to the possibility of radical transformation of that tradition. We see this stance modeled most clearly in Paul's use of scripture. Paul expresses himself, indeed understands himself, through the words and ideas of scripture. Yet he is not bound merely to repeat the sacred texts. He reads God's new work through them so that the texts themselves are transformed. Similarly, we do not abandon our heritage, including the heritage of scripture, but we know that our new circumstances may require new readings and interpretations.

Close attention to Paul's texts enables us to identify their points of tension and their growing edges, and to trace out their trajectories. If I ask what *Paul* meant by "power in weakness" (2 Cor. 12:9) and his "weak," feminine self-presentation, the answer will be primarily an historical one. It will reflect first-century Greco-Roman social constraints, ancient constructions of the body, and so on. But when I consider Paul's notion of power in weakness as a growing edge of his theology and the starting point of a trajectory, I see divine power at work to expose the human construction of what we often think of as "natural" gender roles and characteristics. Paul claims that God's power is shown forth in his weakness. If we take his claim seriously, we will envision leadership differently than society does. Similarly, when Paul says to the Galatians that "all of you are one in Christ Jesus" (Gal. 3:28), we can press beyond the gendered language to understand a "one" that is one human *body*. As such, we are to exhibit not sameness, but the diversity and interdependence that Paul elsewhere (Rom. 12:4–5; 1 Cor. 12:12–27) says characterizes the body of Christ.

Affirming God's work as new creation also means embracing the open-endedness of new creation as a fundamental conviction. We focus precisely on those places where we do not yet see what God will do, but we can affirm that our Creator is still at work. Paul, as a man of his time, was accustomed to using women's "difference" as a reason to circumscribe their activity. On various occasions we see him actually doing so. Yet at other times he treats their leadership as unremarkable (e.g., Rom. 16:1–15, Phil. 4:2, Philem. 2,) or even goes to great lengths to reconcile their Spirit-led activity with the cultural constraints outside of which he cannot think (1 Cor. 11:2–16, on the issue of women's headcovering). Paul lives into the tension created by God's new work in Christ, even when he struggles to describe what this change means (for example, the role of the Law). His letters call us to the same struggle.

Acknowledging My Commitments

Mine is not, of course, the only way to read Paul's letters. Each of the interpretations I have offered in these pages could be countered with others that also make sense of Paul's texts. Any interpretation of these texts is based on certain commitments, choices to make some passages central and ignore or marginalize others, and to trace out some trajectories and leave others aside.

One may decide that the equality of which Paul speaks in texts such as Galatians 3:28 is equality before God, without social implications. Such a stand focuses on Paul's metaphors of redemption and justification and claims that these metaphors present the relationship between the individual and God as most important. This view would see the ethical implications of the gospel as secondary or derivative, though they might remain very important. Paul's ambiguity on social structures and gender roles would serve, in this view, as evidence that Paul did not see social relationships as important to the gospel. This reading of Paul results in a Christian practice that stresses salvation of the soul but ignores or even supports existing societal structures, even if they are discriminatory or oppressive.

It is also possible to see in Paul's writings a sharp division between church and society. This view takes as central Paul's dichotomies, such as flesh and spirit, and traces out the dichotomizing trajectory. What is outside the community, outside the church, is not part of Christian concern. How men and women relate in the church matters; the structures of society not. This way of reading Paul results in a community that is prope described as *sectarian*; its overriding concern is for its own members.

These are only two of the many directions that a reading of Paul might take. My own reading, as I have shown, takes new creation as its central conviction and traces it out in a direction that regards all persons as created in the divine image. I regard Paul's statements of indifference to the present social order not as a principle, but as an element of Paul's interim ethic that needs to be set aside to transform it into an enduring ethic. My reading envisions the church's task as living into the new creation by embodying a radical shift in the ways human beings treat one another and the created order. These are commitments I bring to the reading of Paul, but these commitments have themselves been formed by my reading of the texts and my experience in a Christian community formed by the texts. I have chosen this reading, but I am also shaped by it, and I experience this commitment as a religious calling.

Bearing with Paul

Indeed, the experience of calling is another way I identify with the Paul I find in these texts and see his reported experience as instructive for my own. Paul understands himself to be called by God to a particular task. His theological stance, I would argue, comes out of his experience of calling, and not vice versa: Paul is utterly certain that God intends that the Gentiles come to faith in Christ, despite scant support in scripture, because he knows himself to be called to be apostle to the Gentiles.[4] This certainty gives Paul's mission, and his letters, a strong focal point. The fact that he pays less attention to other issues, or seems ambivalent about them, is the result of his single-minded commitment to the task of breaking down the dividing wall between Jew and Gentile (to use the metaphor from Eph. 2:14). As I have argued earlier, we take Paul's writings most seriously when we commit ourselves to our particular calling—say, to gender or racial equality—as resolutely as he did to his.

Paul's example is also instructive because it is tied to concrete situations, real communities in specific circumstances. Paul is neither a philosopher nor a systematic theologian. Although a theology grounded in "new creation" could easily shift toward theoretical questions, Paul's letters remain connected with his churches. Even if at times we think Paul compromises too much with the existing order, we are able to see that the proclamation of the new must be worked out among real people, with all sorts of complicating circumstances and competing viewpoints. We recognize that we continue to struggle with living out the inclusive message of the Christian faith when we are confronted with people or communities we might prefer not to include. The texts remind us that we cannot ignore the realities of power relationships. Paul presents himself as a model for imitation, and those today who claim roles of church leadership must take responsibility for the power they exercise as well.

Of course, as feminist interpreters in particular have pointed out, when Paul presents himself as a model for imitation it is not necessarily for the empowerment of his readers. Elizabeth Castelli has described how Paul's calls for imitation are claims of unique authority, placing himself in a position of power over his congregations.[5] As we have seen, Paul is a skilled rhetorician who regularly uses the negative tools in his rhetorical arsenal: silencing, "othering," shaming, and the like. Even as he counsels forbearance, he repeatedly refuses to acknowledge the validity of the viewpoints of his partners in conversation. Instead, he styles them as opponents of both himself and "his" gospel. His own situation and practices sometimes blind him to other options. For example, he counsels for singleness and warns against marriage (1 Cor. 7:32–38) despite clear evidence that he knows and appreciates the contributions of ministering couples. And as we have seen in the Pauline tradition in the pastorals, sound theological principles (God as savior of all, the goodness of creation) can easily coexist with destructive ones (restriction of gender roles to mirror those of a highly stratified society). Thus we are able to learn from Paul's careful compromises and his unquestioned assumptions, as well as his blazing insights. To see Paul work out his gospel is regularly to see him fall short of full expression of the principles he professes.

Yet this struggle is itself part of the Christian calling—if, with Paul, we image it not as passive suffering or futile exertion but as productive work, labor to bring new creation to birth. Paul stands in a tradition that he understands to be God's good gift even as he understands that tradition to be radically transformed by God's new act in Christ. He tries to imagine how this new life will actually be lived by real people in real communities as part of real societies (not just a select group in isolation from the rest of the world). The assumptions that he makes about how the structure of those societies works, how "the world is," are not the same assumptions we make today. But we share with Paul the root conviction that God has acted in Christ and that our responsibility is to bring that reality to bear on "the world as it is." The task is not easy, nor is it quickly accomplished. We labor with pain and groaning to see the new creation birthed. It will take all our nurturing skills to make it reality.

Notes

Introduction: Paul and the Female Reader

[1]Rosemary Radford Ruether, *Sexism and God-Talk: Toward a Feminist Theology* (Boston: Beacon Press, 1983), 216–34.

[2]Katherine Doob Sakenfeld, "Feminist Uses of Biblical Materials," in *Feminist Interpretation of the Bible*, ed. Letty M. Russell (Philadelphia: Westminster Press, 1985), 56.

[3]Carolyn Osiek, "The Feminist and the Bible: Hermeneutical Alternatives," in *Feminist Perspectives on Biblical Scholarship*, ed. Adela Yarbro Collins (Chico, Calif.: Scholars Press, 1985), 99.

[4]Mary Ann Tolbert, "Defining the Problem: The Bible and Feminist Hermeneutics," *Semeia* 28 (1984): 114–15.

[5]Osiek, "Feminist and the Bible," 100–101.

[6]Sakenfeld, "Feminist Uses," 59.

[7]Ruether, *Sexism and God-Talk*, 232–34.

[8]Daniel Boyarin, "The Politics of Biblical Narratology: Reading the Bible Like/As a Woman," *Diacritics* 20.4 (Winter 1990): 31.

[9]Ibid., 40.

[10]Antoinette Clark Wire, *The Corinthian Women Prophets: A Reconstruction through Paul's Rhetoric* (Minneapolis: Fortress Press, 1990).

[11]Margaret Y. MacDonald, "Reading Real Women Through the Undisputed Letters of Paul," in *Women and Christian Origins*, ed. Ross Shepard Kraemer and Mary Rose D'Angelo (New York and Oxford: Oxford Univ. Press, 1999), 218.

[12]Ross Shepard Kraemer, ed., *Maenads, Martyrs, Matrons, Monastics: A Sourcebook on Women's Religions in the Greco-Roman World* (Philadelphia: Fortress Press, 1988).

[13]Bernadette J. Brooten, *Women Leaders in the Ancient Synagogue: Inscriptional Evidence and Background Issues* (Chico, Calif.: Scholars Press, 1982).

[14]Boyarin, "Politics of Biblical Narratology," 36.

[15]Elisabeth Schüssler Fiorenza, *In Memory of Her: A Feminist Theological Reconstruction of Christian Origins* (New York: Crossroad, 1992), 213.

[16]Ibid., 226.

[17]Elisabeth Schüssler Fiorenza, Ann Brock and Shelly Matthews, eds., *Searching the Scriptures, Volume Two: A Feminist Commentary* (New York: Crossroad, 1994). The first volume is subtitled *A Feminist Introduction* and consists of essays setting methods and agenda for feminist biblical interpretation.

[18]Ibid., 197.

[19]Catherine Clark Kroeger and Mary J. Evans, eds., *The IVP Women's Bible Commentary* (Downers Grove, Ill.: InterVarsity Press, 2002).

[20]Elizabeth A. Castelli, *Imitating Paul: A Discourse of Power*, Literary Currents in Biblical Interpretation (Louisville: Westminster/John Knox Press, 1991).

[21]See Susan Brooks Thistlethwaite, "Every Two Minutes: Battered Women and Feminist Interpretation," in Russell, *Feminist Interpretation*, 96–107.

Chapter 1: Paul the Man

[1]David J. A. Clines, "Paul the Invisible Man," in *New Testament Masculinities*, ed. Stephen D. Moore and Janice Capel Anderson, Semeia Studies 45 (Atlanta: Society of Biblical Literature, 2003), 182–92.

[2]Clines, 182–92. What follows is a very brief summary of Clines's points.

[3]There exists in some of the world's societies a procedure of female genital cutting, sometimes called "circumcision." This is not, however, the practice under discussion between Paul and his opponents in Galatians, where "circumcision" refers specifically to the removal of the foreskin of the penis and is, obviously, performed on males alone.

[4]See further, chapter 5, pages 78–79.

[5]Paul, apparently, does not see this new status as negating the fact of his Jewishness—he remains a Jew—but only the distinction (apparently, from a divine point of view) that comes with it. On the meaning of this loss of distinction Paul is notoriously unclear. For a cogent argument that Paul does, in spite of himself, negate his Jewish identity, see Daniel Boyarin, *A Radical Jew: Paul and the Politics of Identity* (Berkeley: Univ. of California Press, 1994).

[6]See E. P. Sanders, *Jewish Law from Jesus to the Mishnah: Five Studies* (Philadelphia: Trinity Press International, 1990), 272–83. Despite the clarity of the biblical kosher laws, apparently Diaspora Jews frequently found it acceptable to violate them rather than go without food. The fact that these were treated as "exceptions" seems to reinforce, rather than dilute, the stress on keeping the kosher laws whenever it was within one's power to do so.

[7]Male slaves generally served at those banquets that were attended by males only. Male slaves likely participated in the food preparation necessary for large aristocratic households, although this would have been overseen by the *materfamilias*. Women, rich or poor, were understood to be responsible for the domestic work of the household, whether or not they also participated in trade or public commerce. See Carolyn Osiek and David L. Balch, *Families in the New Testament World: Households and House Churches,* The Family, Religion, and Culture (Louisville: Westminster John Knox Press, 1997), 27–29, 54–60.

[8]Thomas Laqueur, *Making Sex: Body and Gender from the Greeks to Freud* (Cambridge, Mass.: Harvard Univ. Press, 1990), 25–62.

[9]Ibid., 4–5, notes that the Greek language has no separate terms for female sexual organs. The word used to refer to ovaries, for example, is the same as that for testicles.

[10]Dale B. Martin, *The Corinthian Body* (New Haven: Yale Univ. Press, 1995), 248–49.

[11]Most recently, "'The Disease of Effemination': The Charge of Effeminacy and the Verdict of God (Romans 1:18—2:16)," in *New Testament Masculinities,* ed. Stephen D. Moore and Janice Capel Anderson, Semeia Studies 45 (Atlanta: Society of Biblical Literature, 2003), 193–234; and "Sexy Stoics and the Rereading of Romans 1:18—2:16," in *A Feminist Companion to Paul,* ed. Amy-Jill Levine with Marianne Blickenstaff (Cleveland: Pilgrim Press, 2004), 42–73.

[12]See Ross Shepard Kraemer, *Her Share of the Blessings: Women's Religions among Pagans, Jews, and Christians in the Greco-Roman World* (New York and Oxford: Oxford Univ. Press, 1992); *Maenads, Martyrs, Matrons, Monastics: A Sourcebook on Women's Religions in the Greco-Roman World* (Philadelphia: Fortress Press, 1988).

[13]Origen, *Against Celsus,* trans. Alexander Roberts and James Donaldson, Ante-Nicene Christian Library (Edinburgh: T. & T. Clark, 1872), 3.44.

[14]Mary Rose D'Angelo, "(Re)presentations of Women in the Gospel of Matthew and Luke-Acts," in *Women and Christian Origins,* ed. Ross Shepard Kraemer and Mary Rose D'Angelo (New York and Oxford: Oxford Univ. Press, 1999), 181–87.

[15]Carolyn Osiek, "Galatians," *Women's Bible Commentary,* expanded ed., ed. Carol A. Newsom and Sharon H. Ringe (Louisville: Westminster John Knox Press, 1992, 1998), 426.

[16]Beverly R. Gaventa, "The Maternity of Paul," in *The Conversation Continues: Studies in Paul and John in Honor of J. Louis Martyn,* ed. Robert T. Fortna and Beverly R. Gaventa (Nashville: Abingdon Press, 1990), 191, 194.

[17]Gaventa, "Our Mother St. Paul: Toward the Recovery of a Neglected Theme," *Princeton Seminary Bulletin* 17 (1996): 30–37.

[18]Quoted in ibid., 29.

[19]Gaventa, "The Maternity of Paul," 199.

Chapter 2: The World of Paul's Readers

[1]Both these statements are my summaries of the viewpoints of various books and articles. For a comprehensive discussion of this topic, including a list of texts that represent the viewpoints described, see Kathleen E. Corley, *Women and the Historical Jesus: Feminist Myths of Christian Origins* (Sonoma, Calif.: Polebridge, 2002), or her earlier article, "Feminist Myths of Christian Origins," in *Reimagining Christian Origins: A Colloquium Honoring Burton L. Mack,* ed. Elizabeth A. Castelli and Hal Taussig (Valley Forge, Pa.: Trinity Press International, 1996), 51–67.

[2]For an extensive discussion, particularly of the extent to which the Pharisees themselves observed purity regulations, see E. P. Sanders, "Did the Pharisees Eat Ordinary Food in Purity?" in *Jewish Law from Jesus to the Mishnah: Five Studies* (Philadelphia: Trinity Press International, 1990), 131–254. For the Pharisees' influence in Jewish society, see also E. P. Sanders, *Judaism: Practice and Belief, 63 BCE—66 CE* (Philadelphia: Trinity Press International, 1992), 448–51.

[3]Corley, "Feminist Myths," 56. See also Ross S. Kraemer, "Jewish Women and Christian Origins: Some Caveats," in *Women and Christian Origins,* ed. Kraemer and Mary Rose D'Angelo (New York: Oxford Univ. Press, 1999), 35–49.

[4]Bernadette J. Brooten, "Early Christian Women and Their Cultural Context: Issues of Method in Historical Reconstruction," in *Feminist Perspectives on Biblical Scholarship,* ed. Adela Yarbro Collins (Chico, Calif.: Scholars Press, 1984), 65–91.

[5]Mary Daly, *Gyn/Ecology: The Metaethics of Radical Feminism* (Boston: Beacon, 1978), 24, cited in Brooten, "Early Christian Women," 67.

[6]Brooten, "Early Christian Women," 67–68.

[7]Wayne Meeks, *The First Urban Christians: The Social World of the Apostle Paul* (New Haven: Yale Univ. Press, 1983).

[8]See especially Ross S. Kraemer, *Her Share of the Blessings: Women's Religions among Pagans, Jews, and Christians in the Greco-Roman World* (New York and Oxford: Oxford Univ. Press, 1992), 10–11.

[9]A fuller discussion of these matters may be found in Lilian Portefaix, *Sisters Rejoice! Paul's Letter to the Philippians and Luke-Acts as Received by First-Century Philippian Women* (Stockholm: Almqvist & Wiksell International, 1988), 10–32.

[10]Ross S. Kraemer, on this point, comments that "There is some evidence that Jews were less likely to practice abortion or to expose unwanted children, or both, though the evidence is not unambiguous." Kraemer, "Jewish Women and Women's Judaism(s) at the Beginning of Christianity," in Kraemer and D'Angelo, *Women and Christian Origins*, 59.

[11]Portefaix (*Sisters Rejoice*, 10) traces the record of this law to Dionysius of Halicarnassus (first century B.C.E.) and notes that it was not changed even during the revision of matrimonial laws by Augustus, whch generally sought to increase the population.

[12]Two types of legal marriage were recognized in the Roman Empire: although authority over a woman's affairs usually transferred to her husband at marriage, there was also a practice in which the father retained legal control.

[13]An exception should be noted in the case of Roman upper-class women and noblewomen, who often retained close ties with their male blood kin after marriage.

[14]Augustan legislation encouraging the production of children exempted a freewoman who had borne three children, or a freedwoman who had borne four, from legal guardianship.

[15]Tiberias (beginning in 14 C.E.) refused the honors of divinity for himself, but encouraged them for his predecessor Augustus. Gaius (a.k.a. Caligula) demanded that he be regarded as divine, although such honors were not extended to him after his death. Claudius generally refused divine honors but allowed statues of himself to be set up. Nero deified Claudius and was himself depicted in godlike attire on coins. The same general trend continued through Vespasian and Titus. Domitian (who ruled until 96 C.E.) was the first Roman emperor clearly to require recognition of himself as a divine being.

[16]For a perceptive discussion of the pervasiveness and problems of this view, see Ross S. Kraemer, "Jewish Women and Christian Origins: Some Caveats," in Kraemer and D'Angelo, *Women and Christian Origins*, 35–49.

[17]Bernadette Brooten, *Women Leaders in the Ancient Synagogue: Inscriptional Evidence and Background Issues* (Chico, Calif.: Scholars Press, 1982).

[18]See the discussion in Kraemer, *Her Share*, 193 ff., and the sources referenced there. Kraemer comments, helpfully, that we cannot be certain that the women synagogue officers of some diaspora communities did not perform ritual activities (195).

[19]Ibid., 71.

[20]Lynn R. LiDonnici, "Women's Religions and Religious Lives in the Greco-Roman City," in Kraemer and D'Angelo, *Women and Christian Origins*, 88–89. See also Ross Shepard Kraemer, ed., *Maenads, Martyrs, Matrons, Monastics: A Sourcebook on Women's Religions in the Greco-Roman World* (Philadelphia: Fortress Press, 1988), 354–59.

[21]Kraemer, *Her Share*, 79.

[22]For further information on the women described briefly here, see Margaret Y. MacDonald, "Reading Real Women Through the Undisputed Letters of Paul," in Kraemer and D'Angelo, *Women and Christian Origins*, 200–210.

[23]It should be noted, as well, that Acts 16:12–15, 40 gives primary credit for the establishment of the Philippian congregation to a woman, Lydia.

[24]As with Junia (Rom. 16:7; see discussion below), some translators have read Νυμφαν as the masculine name Νύμφας rather than the feminine name Νύμφα; the best manuscript evidence, however, is in favor of the feminine possessive pronoun (*her* house) rather than the masculine.

[25]The address goes on to include also "the church in your house" (τῇ κατ᾽ οἶκόν σου ἐκκλησία); the "you" here is singular, although it is unclear to which of the named individuals the "you" refers.

[26]Joseph A. Fitzmyer, *The Letter to Philemon: A New Translation with Introduction and Commentary*, Anchor Bible 34C (New York: Doubleday, 2000), 87.

[27]Ibid., 87–88.

[28]Ibid., 81.

²⁹Sabine Bieberstein, "Disrupting the Normal Reality of Slavery: A Feminist Reading of the Letter to Philemon," *JSNT* 79 (2000): 106.

³⁰Some interpreters hold that Romans 16 was added to the letter when it was delivered elsewhere than Rome, commenting that it seems unlikely that Paul would know so many people in a church that he had never visited. Phoebe's role, though, is not dependent on the Roman congregation being the recipient of chapter 16. She is commended to whoever receives the letter, and they are asked to offer her hospitality.

³¹It is likely that the scandal of applying the title "apostle" to a woman drove early interpreters, and many after them, to insist that the accusative case form Ἰουνιᾶν derived from a masculine name "Junias," nowhere else attested in ancient literature or inscriptions, rather than the feminine (and common) name "Junia."

Chapter 3: Paul and His Churches

¹The number of house churches in Corinth is debated. Paul seems to address them as a whole, however, and their precise number or composition is not of primary importance to us.

²Antoinette Clark Wire, *The Corinthian Women Prophets: A Reconstruction Through Paul's Rhetoric* (Minneapolis: Fortress Press, 1990).

³See the discussion in Jouette Bassler, "1 Corinthians," in *Women's Bible Commentary*, ed. Carol A. Newsom and Sharon H. Ringe (Louisville: Westminster/John Knox Press, 1992, 1998), 413.

⁴The text on slavery, 7:21, is notoriously unclear and vigorously debated; does Paul mean to say that a slave should gain his or her freedom if possible (NIV, NASB), or *not* accept the opportunity to become free even if that opportunity presents itself (NRSV)?

⁵For an in-depth discussion of these issues, see Margaret Y. MacDonald, "Real Women Through the Undisputed Letters of Paul," in *Women and Christian Origins*, ed. Ross Shepard Kraemer and Mary Rose D'Angelo (New York and Oxford: Oxford Univ. Press, 1999), 199–220, and the sources cited there.

⁶Cited in Lilian Portefaix, *Sisters Rejoice! Paul's Letter to the Philippians and Luke-Acts as Received by First-Century Philippian Women* (Stockholm: Almqvist & Wiksell International, 1988), 17–18.

⁷It should be noted that all these regulations concerning marriage, and logically all of Paul's and other early Christians' discussion of marriage as well, would have applied only to freeborn or freed members of the congregation. Legal marriage was not recognized among slaves in the Roman Empire. Although slaves, of course, entered into sexual relationships, often with mutual commitment, these were not legally binding and could be violated by a master who sought sexual relations with a slave or who chose to sell slave partners away from one another, or children away from their parents.

⁸There was, apparently, a "spiritual marriage" in the early Christian church by which a couple lived together but without sexual relations. This seems to have been a relatively rare occurrence, in any case understood by Paul as possible only for those who had a special gift for it. Some scholars think this is the situation presumed by Paul in 1 Corinthians 7:36–38. See William F. Orr and James Arthur Walther, *I Corinthians*, Anchor Bible 32 (New York: Doubleday, 1976), 223, and the literature cited there.

⁹There was a type of marriage in which the woman remained legally under the control of her father, but this seems to have been an issue when the woman would have been a significant heir. It is not clear how much this would have been practiced in the mostly less-affluent communities of Paul's churches.

¹⁰Similarly, as feminist interpreters have pointed out, the syntactically parallel call for marital partners to grant each other conjugal rights (7:3–4) disguises the quite different significance that delivering one's own body to one's partner for sexual satisfaction would have for women and for men. See Elizabeth A. Castelli, "Paul on Women and Gender," in Kraemer and D'Angelo, *Women and Christian Origins*, 228, and the literature cited there.

¹¹Although some commentators hold that this section is an interpolation; see below.

¹²See the extensive discussion of Dale B. Martin, *The Corinthian Body* (New Haven and London: Yale Univ. Press, 1995), 233–49.

¹³The hierarchy is clearer, of course, if put in order:

> God is to Christ as
> Christ is to man as
> man is to woman.

Paul is not primarily concerned with *establishing* the hierarchical argument, though, but with *using* it to prove his own assertion.

¹⁴This is the view, for example, of Bart Ehrman, in his popular New Testament introduction (Bart D. Ehrman, *The New Testament: A Historical Introduction to the Early Christian Writings*, 3rd ed.

[New York: Oxford Univ. Press, 2004], 402–3). See also Richard Hays, *First Corinthians,* Interpretation: A Bible Commentary for Teaching and Preaching (Louisville: John Knox Press, 1977), 245–49; and the discussion in Carolyn Osiek and David L. Balch, *Families in the New Testament World: Households and House Churches* (Louisville: Westminster John Knox Press, 1997), 117.

[15]Wire, *The Corinthian Women Prophets.*

[16]See William F. Orr and James Arthur Walther, *I Corinthians,* Anchor Bible 32 (New York: Doubleday, 1976), 313.

[17]In Greek, ἥ, the letter *eta* with a smooth breathing mark and an acute accent.

[18]In Greek, ἦ, also the letter *eta* with a smooth breathing mark, but with a circumflex accent.

[19]Several commentators have argued this position; see, most recently, Michel Gourgues, "Who Is Misogynist: Paul or Certain Corinthians? Note on 1 Corinthians 14:33b–36," in Gérald Caron, et al., *Women Also Journeyed with Him: Feminist Perspectives on the Bible* (Collegeville, Minn.: Liturgical, 2000), 117–24, and the extensive literature citations there.

[20]Ross Shepard Kraemer, *Her Share of the Blessings: Women's Religions among Pagans, Jews, and Christians in the Greco-Roman World* (New York and Oxford: Oxford Univ. Press, 1992), 139.

[21]Kraemer points to two neglected New Testament traditions, besides Paul, that may have some bearing on the issue of women's leadership (*Her Share,* 176). In Revelation 2:20, the author denounces the teaching of a false prophetess he tags "Jezebel"; but it is the content of her teaching, not the fact that she taught, that the author of Revelation finds problematic. The second tradition is the "elect lady" to whom 2 John is written. Although most modern scholars assume that the "lady" is the personification of the church, it is striking to discover that Clement of Alexandria, writing less than two centuries after the letter's composition, assumes that it was written to a particular woman, and then by extension to the church (see note 19 in *Her Share,* 243). As Elisabeth Schüssler Fiorenza has pointed out in *In Memory of Her: A Feminist Theological Reconstruction of Christian Origins* (New York: Crossroad, 1992), 248–9, if we do not assume *a priori* that a woman could not have headed a church in Asia, we must concede that the reading that makes this addressee a particular, real woman is inherently plausible.

[22]Recall that letters from Paul to individual churches would have been hand-copied for distribution to other congregations, and it is quite reasonable to imagine that several short letters would have been copied together onto a single scroll for convenience's sake. For various partition theories of 2 Corinthians, see Hans Dieter Betz, *2 Corinthians 8 and 9: A Commentary on Two Administrative Letters of the Apostle Paul,* Hermeneia (Philadelphia: Fortress Press, 1985), 3–35, and the literature cited there.

[23]As in Betz; see note 22.

[24]Paul represents this conflict as fomented by a single individual (2 Cor. 2:5–7), but it is worth questioning whether Paul may be rhetorically minimizing the opposition to him in the congregation by referring to his opposition in the singular.

[25]Other scholars identify 2 Corinthians 10—13 as the "letter of tears," and therefore place it chronologically before 2 Corinthians 1—9; see, e.g., David G. Horrell, *The Social Ethos of the Corinthian Correspondence: Interests and Ideology From 1 Corinthians to 1 Clement,* Studies of the New Testament and Its World (Edinburgh: T&T Clark, 1996). Such a proposal has much to commend it, including the attractive possibility that our information about the Corinthian congregation ends on the positive note of Paul's reconciliation with them, but in my view the proposal has serious flaws as well.

[26]See the evidence marshaled by Jennifer Larson that hearers evaluated a rhetorician's presentation by criteria expressly equated with his masculinity: Larson, "Paul's Masculinity," *JBL* 123/1 (2004): 87–94.

[27]Ibid., 96.

Chapter 4: No Male and Female

[1]Brigitte Kahl, "No Longer Male: Masculinity Struggles Behind Galatians 3:28?" *JSNT* 79 (2000): 40.

[2]Wayne Meeks, "The Image of the Androgyne: Some Uses of a Symbol in Earliest Christianity," *History of Religions* 13 (1974): 182.

[3]Aristotle, *Metaphysics* 986a, cited in J. Louis Martyn, *Galatians: A New Translation with Introduction and Commentary,* Anchor Bible 33A (New York: Doubleday, 1997), 376.

[4]Elisabeth Schüssler Fiorenza, *In Memory of Her: A Feminist Theological Reconstruction of Christian Origins* (New York: Crossroad, 1992), 211.

[5]See Sheila Briggs, "Galatians," in *Searching the Scriptures, Vol. 2, A Feminist Commentary,* ed. Elisabeth Schüssler Fiorenza, with Ann Brock and Shelly Matthews (New York: Crossroad, 1994), 219.

[6]See Dennis R. MacDonald, *There Is No Male and Female: The Fate of a Dominical Saying in Paul and Gnosticism,* Harvard Dissertations in Religion (Philadelphia: Fortress Press, 1987).

[7]Schüssler Fiorenza, *In Memory of Her,* 213.

[8]Kahl, "No Longer Male," 37.

[9]Daniel Boyarin, *A Radical Jew: Paul and the Politics of Identity* (Berkeley, Los Angeles, London: Univ. of California Press, 1994), 181.

[10]Dieter Lührmann, *Galatians: A Continental Commentary,* Continental Commentaries, trans. O. C. Dean, Jr. (Minneapolis: Fortress Press, 1992), 77.

[11]See the summary of possible interpretations of Gal. 3:28 listed by Carolyn Osiek, "Galatians," in *Women's Bible Commentary,* ed. Carol A. Newsom and Sharon H. Ringe, expanded ed. (Louisville: Westminster/John Knox Press, 1992, 1998), 425. A similar, but more extended discussion of various interpretive possibilities may be found in Mary Rose D'Angelo, "Gender Refusers in the Early Christian Mission: Gal 3:28 as an Interpretation of Gen 1:27b," in *Reading in Christian Communities: Essays on Interpretation in the Early Church,* ed. Charles A. Bobertz and David Brakke (Notre Dame, Ind.: Univ. of Notre Dame Press, 2002), 149–73.

[12]E.g., in 1 Cor. 7:5, 10:8.

[13]MacDonald, "Reading Real Women," in *Women and Christian Origins,* ed. Ross Shepard Kraemer and Mary Rose D'Angelo (New York and Oxford: Oxford Univ. Press, 1999), 215.

[14]Krister Stendahl, *The Bible and the Role of Women: A Case Study in Hermeneutics,* Facet Books Biblical Series 15, trans. Emilie T. Sander (Philadelphia: Fortress Press, 1966), 36.

[15]Francis Lyall, *Slaves, Citizens, Sons: Legal Metaphors in the Epistles* (Grand Rapids, Mich: Academie, 1984) cited in Elisabeth Schüssler Fiorenza, *Rhetoric and Ethic: The Politics of Biblical Studies* (Minneapolis: Fortress Press, 1999), 161.

[16]Schüssler Fiorenza, *Rhetoric and Ethic,* 162.

[17]Elizabeth Castelli, "Paul on Women and Gender," in Kraemer and D'Angelo, *Women and Christian Origins,* 230.

[18]Ibid.

[19]Krister Stendahl, "Ancient Scripture in the Modern World," in *Scripture in the Jewish and Christian Traditions: Authority, Interpretation, Relevance,* ed. Frederick E. Greenspahn (Nashville: Abingdon Press, 1982), 208–9.

[20]Boyarin, *A Radical Jew,* 187.

[21]Bonnie Thurston, *Women in the New Testament: Questions and Commentary,* Companions to the New Testament (New York: Crossroad, 1998), 59.

[22]Mary Ann Tolbert, "A New Teaching With Authority," in *Teaching the Bible: The Discourses and Politics of Biblical Pedagogy,* ed. Fernando F. Segovia and Mary Ann Tolbert (Maryknoll, N.Y.: Orbis Books, 1998), 184–85.

[23]Beverly Roberts Gaventa, "Is Galatians Just a 'Guy Thing'? A Theological Reflection," *Interpretation* 54 (2000): 271–72.

[24]Boyarin, *A Radical Jew,* 181.

[25]Amy Plantinga Pauw, "The Word Is Near You: A Feminist Conversation with Lindbeck," *Theology Today* 50 (April 1993): 52.

Chapter 5: Paul the Iconoclast

[1]Essays from the group's meetings were published as Jouette Bassler, ed., *Pauline Theology, Volume I: Thessalonians, Philippians, Galatians, Philemon* (Minneapolis: Fortress Press, 1991); David M. Hay, ed., *Pauline Theology, Volume II: 1 & 2 Corinthians* (Minneapolis: Fortress Press, 1993); David M. Hay and E. Elizabeth Johnson, eds., *Pauline Theology, Volume III: Romans* (Minneapolis: Fortress Press, 1995); and E. Elizabeth Johnson and David M. Hay, eds., *Pauline Theology, Volume IV: Looking Back, Pressing On,* SBL Symposium Series 4 (Atlanta: Scholars Press, 1997). The fourth volume contains four essays evaluating the ten-year "experiment."

[2]J. Christiaan Beker, *Paul the Apostle: The Triumph of God in Life and Thought* (Minneapolis: Fortress Press, 1980), 35.

[3]This word (Χριστιανός) seems to be unknown to Paul, at least as the letters are evidence. It appears in the NT first in Acts 11:26, "…it was in Antioch that the disciples were first called 'Christians.'" Other NT occurrences are Acts 26:28 and 1 Peter 4:16.

[4]Albert Schweitzer, *The Mysticism of Paul the Apostle,* trans. William Montgomery (New York: Henry Holt, 1931), ix.

[5]For elaboration on this theme, see Sandra Hack Polaski, *Paul and the Discourse of Power* (Sheffield: Sheffield Academic Press, 1999).

[6]Elizabeth Castelli, *Imitating Paul: A Discourse of Power,* Literary Currents in Biblical Interpretation (Louisville: Westminster/John Knox Press, 1991).

[7]David J. A. Clines, "Paul the Invisible Man," in *New Testament Masculinities*, ed. Stephen D. Moore and Janice Capel Anderson, Semeia Studies 45 (Atlanta: Society of Biblical Literature, 2003), 182–92.

[8]For a helpful discussion of convictions and how a system of convictions organizes a semantic universe, see Daniel Patte, *Paul's Faith and the Power of the Gospel: A Structural Introduction to the Pauline Letters* (Philadelphia: Fortress Press, 1983), esp. 9–29.

[9]Luzia Sutter Rehmann, "German-Language Feminist Exegesis of the Pauline Letters: A Survey," *JSNT* 79 (2000): 9.

[10]The emphasis on new creation in connection with the apocalyptic nature of Paul's thought is not new; see, for example, J. Louis Martyn, "Apocalyptic Antinomies in Paul's Letter to the Galatians," *NTS* 31:3 (1985): 410–24.

[11]See J. Christiaan Beker, *The Triumph of God: The Essence of Paul's Thought* (Minneapolis: Fortress Press, 1990).

[12]Richard B. Hays, *Echoes of Scripture in the Letters of Paul* (New Haven: Yale Univ. Press, 1989), 44–45.

[13]Ibid., 54–57. A fuller description and nuanced discussion of Paul's use of scripture may be found in *Echoes of Scripture*.

[14]Sheila E. McGinn, "Feminist Approaches to Romans: Rom. 8:18–23 as a Case Study," paper presented in the "Romans Through History and Culture" Seminar, Society for Biblical Literature Annual Meeting, Nashville, Tennessee, 21 November 2000; Elizabeth A. Castelli, "Romans," in *Searching the Scriptures, Volume Two: A Feminist Commentary*, ed. Elisabeth Schüssler Fiorenza, Ann Brock, and Shelly Matthews (New York: Crossroad, 1994), 272–300.

[15]Castelli, "Romans," 286.

[16]McGinn, "Feminist Approaches," 10–11.

[17]Ibid., 18.

[18]On a topic close to the present work, see Pamela Eisenbaum, "Is Paul the Father of Misogyny and Antisemitism?" *Cross Currents* 50 (Winter 2000–01): 506–24; she treats particularly the metaphor of adoption. She joins other Jewish feminist writers, notably Daniel Boyarin, who have engaged the work and thought of their fellow religionist; see especially Daniel Boyarin, *A Radical Jew: Paul and the Politics of Identity* (Berkeley, Los Angeles, London: Univ. of California Press, 1994), and "Paul and the Genealogy of Gender," in Amy-Jill Levine and Marianne Blickenstaff, eds, *A Feminist Companion to Paul* (Cleveland: Pilgrim Press, 2004).

Chapter 6: Interpreters of Paul

[1]See ancient sources cited in David G. Meade, *Pseudonymity and Canon: An Investigation into the Relationship of Authorship and Authority in Jewish and Earliest Christian Tradition* (Grand Rapids: Eerdmans, 1986).

[2]For discussion and bibliography on issues of pseudonymity and the deutero-Pauline writings, see Raymond E. Brown, *An Introduction to the New Testament* (New York: Doubleday, 1997), 585–89, 610–15, 627–30, 662–68, 672–75. Brown claims that 60 percent of scholars regard Colossians as pseudonymous, 70 to 80 percent for Ephesians, and 80 to 90 percent for the pastoral epistles.

Luke Timothy Johnson opts for the Pauline authorship of Colossians and Ephesians and argues that the pastorals give us important information about Paul's missionary work. See Johnson, *The Writings of the New Testament: An Interpretation* (Minneapolis: Fortress Press, 1999), 393–95, 407–12, 423–28.

The remaining seven letters (Romans, 1 and 2 Corinthians, Galatians, Philippians, 1 Thessalonians, Philemon) are designated the "authentic" or "undisputed" letters of Paul. While questions have been raised about the authorship and literary integrity of these texts, very few scholars today would argue that these do not come, except for small portions, from Paul himself.

[3]The address "to the Ephesians" in Eph. 1:1 is missing from several important extant manuscripts, as well as the manuscripts used by some of the church fathers (Basil, Origen), leading some commentators to deduce that this was originally a "general" or encyclical letter, sent to several locations including Ephesus.

[4]See, for example, E. Elizabeth Johnson, "Ephesians," in *Women's Bible Commentary*, ed. Carol A. Newsom and Sharon H. Ringe, expanded ed. (Louisville: Westminster/John Knox Press, 1992, 1998), 430–32; and "Colossians," in *Women's Bible Commentary*, 438–39.

[5]Angela Standhartinger, "The Origin and Intention of the Household Code in the Letter to the Colossians," *JSNT* 79 (2000), 129, argues that ἰσότης in 4:1 is "an interpretive key to reading the code—one that, when taken in context, counters the apparent prevailing subordination-ethos."

⁶E. Elizabeth Johnson, "Ephesians," in Newsom and Ringe, *Women's Bible Commentary,* 431.

⁷On these points, see the argument of Virginia Ramey Mollenkott, "Emancipative Elements in Ephesians 5.21–33: Why Feminist Scholarship Has (Often) Left Them Unmentioned, and Why They Should Be Emphasized," in *A Feminist Companion to the Deutero-Pauline Epistles,* ed. Amy-Jill Levine with Marianne Blickenstaff (Cleveland: Pilgrim Press, 2003), 37–58.

⁸Along these lines it is worth noting that 2 Timothy is written explicitly as a sort of "last will and testament" as Paul is facing martyrdom. Those who do argue for Pauline authorship of the pastorals usually place them all in the later years of Paul's ministry.

⁹Joanna Dewey emphasizes this distinction: "2 Timothy," in Newsom and Ringe, *Women's Bible Commentary,* 445.

¹⁰For an accessible and perceptive discussion of this passage, see Jouette M. Bassler, *1 Timothy, 2 Timothy, Titus,* Abingdon New Testament Commentaries (Nashville: Abingdon Press, 1996), 55–63.

¹¹Ibid., 59.

¹²The NRSV, like the KJV, reflects the odd shift. Other English translations (RSV, HCSB, NIV, REB, NASB) make the subject of the whole verse either singular or plural (NIV and HCSB add a translation note).

¹³See also Jouette M. Bassler, "Limits and Differentiation: The Calculus of Widows in 1 Timothy 5.3–16," in Levine and Blickenstaff, *A Feminist Companion to the Deutero-Pauline Epistles,* 122–46; and Bonnie Thurston, "1 Timothy 5.3–16 and the Leadership of Women in the Early Church," in Levine and Blickenstaff, 159–74.

¹⁴The classic argument of this position may be found in Dennis Ronald MacDonald, *The Legend and the Apostle: The Battle for Paul in Story and Canon* (Philadelphia: Westminster Press, 1983).

¹⁵The text of "The Acts of Paul and Thecla" may be found in *The Apocryphal New Testament,* trans. J. K. Elliott (New York: Oxford University Press, 1993).

¹⁶Elizabeth A. Clark, *Reading Renunciation: Asceticism and Scripture in Early Christianity* (Princeton: Princeton Univ. Press, 1999), 261.

¹⁷Ibid., 263.

¹⁸For a fuller discussion of this topic, with references to the works of the patristic authors mentioned, see chapter 10, "I Corinthians 7 in Early Christian Exegesis," in Clark, *Reading Renunciation,* 259–329.

¹⁹Clark, *Reading Renunciation,* 267.

²⁰Ibid., 269.

²¹Ibid., 318.

²²Ibid., 272.

²³Ibid., 305.

²⁴John Chrysostom, *On Virginity: Against Remarriage,* trans. Sally Rieger Shore, Studies in Women and Religion 9 (New York: Edwin Mellen, 1983), 91–95.

²⁵Clark, *Reading Renunciation,* 300–301.

²⁶Ibid., 316.

²⁷Ibid., 274.

²⁸Ibid., 298.

²⁹Ibid., 295–96.

³⁰Ibid., 283–85.

³¹See, for example, E. P. Sanders, *Paul, the Law, and the Jewish People* (Philadelphia: Fortress Press, 1983).

³²See Ross S. Kraemer, "Jewish Women and Women's Judaism(s) at the Beginning of Christianity," in *Women and Christian Origins,* ed. Ross Shepard Kraemer and Mary Rose D'Angelo (New York and Oxford: Oxford Univ. Press, 1999), 50–79.

Conclusion: Reading Paul Today

¹Alain Badiou, *Saint Paul: The Foundation of Universalism,* trans. Ray Brassier, Cultural Memory in the Present (Stanford, Calif.; Stanford Univ. Press, 2003).

²Mary Ann Tolbert, "A New Teaching with Authority: A Re-evaluation of the Authority of the Bible," in *Teaching the Bible: The Discourses and Politics of Biblical Pedagogy,* ed. Fernando F. Segovia and Mary Ann Tolbert (Maryknoll, N.Y.: Orbis Books, 1998), 183.

³Ibid., 184.

⁴For more extensive discussion see Sandra Hack Polaski, *Paul and the Discourse of Power* (Sheffield: Sheffield Academic Press, 1999), 95–103.

⁵Elizabeth Castelli, *Imitating Paul: A Discourse of Power,* Literary Currents in Biblical Interpretation (Louisville: Westminster/John Knox Press, 1991).

Bibliography

Abrahamsen, Valerie A. *Women and Worship at Philippi: Diana/Artemis and Other Cults in the Early Christian Era*. Portland, Maine: Astarte Shell Press, 1995.

Adam, Margaret B. "This Is *My* Story, This Is *My* Song…: A Feminist Claim on Scripture, Ideology and Interpretation." In *Escaping Eden,* edited by Harold C. Washington et al., 218–32.

Aspegren, Kerstin. *The Male Woman: A Feminine Ideal in the Early Church.* Edited by René Kieffer. Acta Universitatis Upsaliensis, Uppsala Women's Studies, A. Women in Religion 4. Stockholm: Almqvist & Wiksell, 1990.

Badiou, Alain. *Saint Paul: The Foundation of Universalism.* Translated by Ray Brassier. Cultural Memory in the Present. Stanford, Calif.: Stanford Univ. Press, 2003.

Bassler, Jouette M. "1 Corinthians." In *Women's Bible Commentary,* edited by Carol A. Newsom and Sharon H. Ringe, 411–19.

_____. *1 Timothy, 2 Timothy, Titus.* Abingdon New Testament Commentaries. Nashville: Abingdon Press, 1996.

_____. "2 Corinthians." In *Women's Bible Commentary,* edited by Carol A. Newsom and Sharon H. Ringe, 420–22.

_____, ed. *Pauline Theology, Volume I: Thessalonians, Philippians, Galatians, Philemon.* Minneapolis: Fortress Press, 1991.

Beker, J. Christiaan. *Paul the Apostle: The Triumph of God in Life and Thought.* Minneapolis: Fortress Press, 1980.

_____. *The Triumph of God: The Essence of Paul's Thought.* Translated by Loren T. Stuckenbruck. Minneapolis: Fortress Press, 1990.

Belleville, Linda L. *Women Leaders and the Church: Three Crucial Questions.* Grand Rapids: Baker, 2000.

Betz, Hans Dieter. *Galatians: A Commentary on Paul's Letter to the Churches in Galatia.* Hermeneia: A Critical and Historical Commentary on the Bible. Philadelphia: Fortress Press, 1979.

_____. *2 Corinthians 8 and 9: A Commentary on Two Administrative Letters of the Apostle Paul.* Hermeneia: A Critical and Historical Commentary on the Bible. Philadelphia: Fortress Press, 1985.

Bieberstein, Sabine. "Disrupting the Normal Reality of Slavery: A Feminist Reading of the Letter to Philemon." *JSNT* 79 (2000): 105–16.

Bird, Phyllis A. "What Makes a Feminist Reading Feminist? A Qualified Answer." In *Escaping Eden,* edited by Harold C. Washington et al., 124–31.

Boyarin, Daniel. "Paul and the Genealogy of Gender." In *A Feminist Companion to Paul,* edited by Amy-Jill Levine with Marianne Blickenstaff, 13–41.

_____. "The Politics of Biblical Narratology: Reading the Bible Like/As a Woman." *Diacritics* 20.4 (1990): 31–42.

_____. *A Radical Jew: Paul and the Politics of Identity.* Berkeley, Los Angeles, London: Univ. of California Press, 1994.

Briggs, Sheila. "Can an Enslaved God Liberate? Hermeneutical Reflection on Philippians 2:6–11." *Semeia* 47 (1989): 137–53.

_____. "Galatians." In *Searching the Scriptures, Vol. 2,* edited by Elisabeth Schüssler Fiorenza et al., 218–36.

Bristow, John Temple. *What Paul Really Said About Women: An Apostle's Liberating Views on Equality in Marriage, Leadership, and Love.* San Francisco: Harper & Row, 1988.

Brooten, Bernadette J. "Early Christian Women and Their Cultural Context: Issues of Method in Historical Reconstruction." In *Feminist Perspectives on Biblical Scholarship,* edited by Adela Yarbro Collins, 65–92.

_____. *Women Leaders in the Ancient Synagogue: Inscriptional Evidence and Background Issues.* Chico, Calif.: Scholars Press, 1982.

Brown, Raymond E. *An Introduction to the New Testament.* The Anchor Bible Reference Library. New York: Doubleday, 1997.

Caron, Gérald, Aldina da Silva, Olivette Genest, Marc Girard, Michel Gourgues, Élisabeth J. Lacelle, Jean-Jacques Lavoie, André Myre, and Jean-François Racine. *Women Also Journeyed with Him: Feminist Perspectives on the Bible.* Translated by Madeleine Beaumont. Collegeville, Minn.: Liturgical Press, 2000.

Castelli, Elizabeth A. *Imitating Paul: A Discourse of Power.* Literary Currents in Biblical Interpretation. Louisville: Westminster/John Knox Press, 1991.

_____. "Interpretations of Power in 1 Corinthians." *Semeia* 54 (1991): 197–222.

_____. "Paul on Women and Gender." In *Women and Christian Origins,* edited by Ross Shepard Kraemer and Mary Rose D'Angelo, 221–35.

_____. "Romans." In *Searching the Scriptures, Vol. 2,* edited by Elisabeth Schüssler Fiorenza et al., 272–300.

Castelli, Elizabeth A., and Hal Taussig, eds. *Reimagining Christian Origins: A Colloquium Honoring Burton L. Mack.* Valley Forge, Pa.: Trinity Press International, 1996.

Chrysostom, John. *On Virginity; Against Remarriage.* Translated by Sally Rieger Shore. Studies in Women and Religion 9. New York: Edwin Mellen Press, 1983.

Clark, Elizabeth A. *Reading Renunciation: Asceticism and Scripture in Early Christianity.* Princeton: Princeton Univ. Press, 1999.

Clines, David J. A. "Ecce Vir; or, Gendering the Son of Man." In *Biblical Studies, Cultural Studies: The Third Sheffield Colloquium,* edited by J. Cheryl Exum and Stephen D. Moore, 352–75.

_____."Paul, the Invisible Man." In *New Testament Masculinities,* edited by Stephen D. Moore and Janice Capel Anderson, 181–92.

_____. "Play the Man! The Masculine Imperative in the Bible." In *Interested Parties: The Ideology of Writers and Readers of the Hebrew Bible,* 212–41. JSOTSup 205; Gender, Culture, Theory, 1. Sheffield: Sheffield Academic Press, 1995.

Collins, Adela Yarbro, ed. *Feminist Perspectives on Biblical Scholarship.* Chico, Calif.: Scholars Press, 1984.

Corley, Kathleen E. "Feminist Myths of Christian Origins." In *Reimagining Christian Origins: A Colloquium Honoring Burton L. Mack,* edited by Elizabeth A. Castelli and Hal Taussig, 51–67.

_____. *Private Women, Public Meals: Social Conflict in the Synoptic Tradition.* Peabody, Mass.: Hendrickson, 1993.

_____.*Women and the Historical Jesus: Feminist Myths of Christian Origins.* Sonoma, Calif.: Polebridge, 2002.

_____. "Women's Inheritance Rights in Antiquity and Paul's Metaphor of Adoption." In *A Feminist Companion to Paul,* edited by Amy-Jill Levine with Marianne Blickenstaff, 98–121.

D'Angelo, Mary Rose. "Colossians." In *Searching the Scriptures, Vol. 2,* edited by Elisabeth Schüssler Fiorenza et al., 313–24.

_____. "Gender Refusers in the Early Christian Mission: Gal 3:28 as an Interpretation of Gen 1:27b." In *Reading in Christian Communities: Essays on Interpretation in the Early Church,* edited by Charles A. Bobertz and David Brakke, 149–73. Notre Dame, Ind.: Univ. of Notre Dame Press, 2002.

_____. "(Re)presentations of Women in the Gospel of Matthew and Luke-Acts." In *Women and Christian Origins,* edited by Ross Shepard Kraemer and Mary Rose D'Angelo, 171–95.

Davies, Margaret. *The Pastoral Epistles.* New Testament Guides. Sheffield: Sheffield Academic Press, 1996.

Dewey, Joanna. "1 Timothy." In *Women's Bible Commentary,* edited by Carol A. Newsom and Sharon H. Ringe, 444–49.

_____."2 Timothy." In *Women's Bible Commentary,* edited by Carol A. Newsom and Sharon H. Ringe, 450–51.

_____."Titus." In *Women's Bible Commentary,* edited by Carol A. Newsom and Sharon H. Ringe, 452.

Ehrman, Bart D. *The New Testament: A Historical Introduction to the Early Christian Writings.* 3rd ed. New York: Oxford Univ. Press, 2004.

Eisen, Ute E. *Women Officeholders in Early Christianity: Epigraphical and Literary Studies.* Translated by Linda M. Maloney. Collegeville, Minn.: Liturgical Press, 2000.

Eisenbaum, Pamela. "Is Paul the Father of Misogyny and Antisemitism?" *Cross Currents* 50 (Winter 2000–01): 506–24.

Elliott, J. K., trans. *The Apocryphal New Testament.* New York: Oxford Univ. Press, 1993.

Exum, J. Cheryl, and Stephen D. Moore, eds. *Biblical Studies, Cultural Studies: The Third Sheffield Colloquium.* JSOTSup 266; Gender, Culture, Theory 7. Sheffield: Sheffield Academic Press, 1998.

Farley, Margaret A. "Feminist Consciousness and the Interpretation of Scripture." In *Feminist Interpretation of the Bible,* edited by Letty M. Russell, 41–51.

Fatum, Lone. "1 Thessalonians." In *Searching the Scriptures, Vol. 2,* edited by Elisabeth Schüssler Fiorenza et al., 250–62.

Fitzmyer, Joseph A. *The Letter to Philemon: A New Translation with Introduction and Commentary.* Anchor Bible 34C. New York: Doubleday, 2000.

Fortna, Robert T., and Beverly R. Gaventa, eds. *The Conversation Continues: Studies in Paul and John in Honor of J. Louis Martyn.* Nashville: Abingdon Press, 1990.

Gaventa, Beverly Roberts. "Is Galatians Just a 'Guy Thing'? A Theological Reflection." *Interpretation* 54 (2000): 267–78.

_____. "The Maternity of Paul: An Exegetical Study of Galatians 4:19." In *The Conversation Continues: Studies in Paul and John in Honor of J. Louis Martyn,* edited by Robert T. Fortna and Beverly R. Gaventa, 189–201.

_____. "Our Mother St. Paul: Toward the Recovery of a Neglected Theme." *Princeton Seminary Bulletin* 17 (1996): 29–44. Reprinted in *A Feminist Companion to Paul,* edited by Amy-Jill Levine with Marianne Blickenstaff, 85–97.

_____. "Romans." In *Women's Bible Commentary,* edited by Carol A. Newsom and Sharon H. Ringe, 403–10.

Gourgues, Michel. "Who Is Misogynist: Paul or Certain Corinthians? Note on 1 Corinthians 14:33b–36." In *Women also Journeyed with Him,* edited by Gérald Caron et al., 117–24.

Greenspahn, Frederick E., ed. *Scripture in the Jewish and Christian Traditions: Authority, Interpretation, Relevance.* Nashville: Abingdon Press, 1982.

Gryson, Roger. *The Ministry of Women in the Early Church.* Translated by Jean Laporte and Mary Louise Hall. Collegeville, Minn.: Liturgical Press, 1976.

Gundry-Volf, Judith. "Christ and Gender: A Study of Difference and Equality in Gal 3:28." In *Jesus Christus als de Mitte der Schrift: Studien zur Hermeneutik des Evangeliums,* edited by Christof Landmesser et al., 439–77. Berlin and New York: Walter de Gruyter, 1997.

Hay, David M., ed. *Pauline Theology, Volume II: 1 & 2 Corinthians.* Minneapolis: Fortress Press, 1993.

Hay, David M., and E. Elizabeth Johnson, eds. *Pauline Theology, Volume III: Romans.* Minneapolis: Fortress Press, 1995.

Hays, Richard B. *Echoes of Scripture in the Letters of Paul.* New Haven and London: Yale Univ. Press, 1989.

_____. *First Corinthians.* Interpretation: A Bible Commentary for Teaching and Preaching. Louisville: John Knox Press, 1997.

Heine, Susanne. *Women and Early Christianity: A Reappraisal.* Translated by John Bowden. Minneapolis: Augsburg Publishing House, 1988.

Johnson, E. Elizabeth. "Colossians." In *Women's Bible Commentary,* edited by Carol A. Newsom and Sharon H. Ringe, 437–39.

_____. "Ephesians." In *Women's Bible Commentary,* edited by Carol A. Newsom and Sharon H. Ringe, 428–32.

Johnson, E. Elizabeth, and David M. Hay, eds. *Pauline Theology, Volume IV: Looking Back, Pressing On.* SBL Symposium Series 4. Atlanta: Scholars Press, 1997.

Johnson, Luke Timothy. *The Writings of the New Testament: An Interpretation.* Rev. ed. Minneapolis: Fortress Press, 1999.

Kahl, Brigitte. "No Longer Male: Masculinity Struggles Behind Galatians 3:28?" *JSNT* 79 (2000): 37–49.

Knox, John. *Philemon Among the Letters of Paul: A New View of Its Place and Importance.* Rev. ed. Nashville: Abingdon Press, 1959.

Kraemer, Ross Shepard. *Her Share of the Blessings: Women's Religions among Pagans, Jews, and Christians in the Greco-Roman World.* New York and Oxford: Oxford Univ. Press, 1992.

_____. "Jewish Women and Christian Origins: Some Caveats." In *Women and Christian Origins,* edited by Ross Shepard Kraemer and Mary Rose D'Angelo, 35–49.

_____. "Jewish Women and Women's Judaism(s) at the Beginning of Christianity." In *Women and Christian Origins,* edited by Ross Shepard Kraemer and Mary Rose D'Angelo, 50–79.

_____, ed. *Maenads, Martyrs, Matrons, Monastics: A Sourcebook on Women's Religions in the Greco-Roman World.* Philadelphia: Fortress Press, 1988.

Kraemer, Ross Shepard, and Mary Rose D'Angelo, eds. *Women and Christian Origins.* New York and Oxford: Oxford Univ. Press, 1999.

Kroeger, Catherine Clark, and Mary J. Evans, eds. *The IVP Women's Bible Commentary.* Downers Grove, Ill.: InterVarsity Press, 2002.

Lampe, Peter. "The Roman Christians of Romans 16." In *The Romans Debate*, edited by Karl P. Donfried. Rev. ed., 216–30. Peabody, Mass.: Hendrickson, 1991.

Laqueur, Thomas. *Making Sex: Body and Gender from the Greeks to Freud.* Cambridge, Mass.: Harvard Univ. Press, 1990.

Larson, Jennifer. "Paul's Masculinity." *JBL* 123/1 (2004): 85–97.

Lefkowitz, Mary R., and Maureen B. Fant. *Women's Life in Greece and Rome: A Source Book in Translation.* 2d ed. Baltimore: Johns Hopkins Univ. Press, 1982, 1992.

Levine, Amy-Jill, with Marianne Blickenstaff, eds. *A Feminist Companion to Paul.* Cleveland: Pilgrim Press, 2004.

_____, eds. *A Feminist Companion to the Deutero-Pauline Epistles.* Cleveland: Pilgrim Press, 2003.

LiDonnici, Lynn R. "Women's Religions and Religious Lives in the Greco-Roman City." In *Women and Christian Origins,* edited by Ross Shepard Kraemer and Mary Rose D'Angelo, 80–102.

Lührmann, Dieter. *Galatians: A Continental Commentary.* Continental Commentaries. Translated by O. C. Dean, Jr. Minneapolis: Fortress Press, 1992.

MacDonald, Dennis Ronald. *The Legend and the Apostle: The Battle for Paul in Story and Canon.* Philadelphia: Westminster Press, 1983.

_____. *There Is No Male and Female: The Fate of a Dominical Saying in Paul and Gnosticism.* Harvard Dissertations in Religion. Philadelphia: Fortress Press, 1987.

MacDonald, Margaret Y. *Early Christian Women and Pagan Opinion: The Power of the Hysterical Woman.* Cambridge: Cambridge Univ. Press, 1996.

_____. "Reading Real Women Through the Undisputed Letters of Paul." In *Women and Christian Origins,* edited by Ross Shepard Kraemer and Mary Rose D'Angelo, 199–220.

_____. "Rereading Paul: Early Interpreters of Paul on Women and Gender." In *Women and Christian Origins,* edited by Ross Shepard Kraemer and Mary Rose D'Angelo, 236–53.

Maloney, Linda M. "The Pastoral Epistles." In *Searching the Scriptures, Vol. 2,* edited by Elisabeth Schüssler Fiorenza et al., 361–80.

Martin, Dale B. *The Corinthian Body.* New Haven and London: Yale Univ. Press, 1995.

Martyn, J. Louis. "Apocalyptic Antinomies in Paul's Letter to the Galatians." *NTS* 31:3 (1985): 410–24.

_____. *Galatians: A New Translation with Introduction and Commentary.* Anchor Bible 33A. New York: Doubleday, 1997.

Matthews, Shelly. *First Converts: Rich Pagan Women and the Rhetoric of Mission in Early Judaism and Christianity.* Contraversions. Stanford: Stanford Univ. Press, 2001.

_____. "2 Corinthians." In *Searching the Scriptures, Vol. 2,* edited by Elisabeth Schüssler Fiorenza et al., 196–217.

McGinn, Sheila E. "The Acts of Thecla." In *Searching the Scriptures, Vol. 2,* edited by Elisabeth Schüssler Fiorenza et al., 800–828.

_____. "Feminist Approaches to Romans: Rom. 8:18–23 as a Case Study." Paper presented in the "Romans Through History and Culture" Seminar, Society for Biblical Literature Annual Meeting, Nashville, Tenn., 21 November 2000.

Meade, David G. *Pseudonymity and Canon: An Investigation into the Relationship of Authorship and Authority in Jewish and Earliest Christian Tradition.* Grand Rapids: Eerdmans, 1986.

Meeks, Wayne A. *The First Urban Christians: The Social World of the Apostle Paul.* New Haven: Yale Univ. Press, 1983.

_____. "The Image of the Androgyne: Some Uses of a Symbol in Earliest Christianity." *History of Religions* 13 (1974): 165–79.

Mitchell, Margaret M. *Paul and the Rhetoric of Reconciliation: An Exegetical Investigation of the Language and Composition of 1 Corinthians.* Louisville: Westminster/John Knox Press, 1993.

Moore, Stephen D., and Janice Capel Anderson, eds. *New Testament Masculinities.* Semeia Studies 45. Atlanta: Society of Biblical Literature, 2003.

Newsom, Carol A., and Sharon H. Ringe, eds. *Women's Bible Commentary.* Expanded ed. Louisville: Westminster John Knox Press, 1992, 1998.

Orr, William F., and James Arthur Walther. *I Corinthians: A New Translation; Introduction with a Study of the Life of Paul, Notes, and Commentary.* Anchor Bible 32. New York: Doubleday, 1976.

Osiek, Carolyn. "The Feminist and the Bible: Hermeneutical Alternatives." In *Feminist Perspectives on Biblical Scholarship,* edited by Adela Yarbro Collins, 93–106.

_____. "Galatians." In *Women's Bible Commentary,* edited by Carol A. Newsom and Sharon H. Ringe, 423–27.

_____. "Philippians." In *Searching the Scriptures, Vol. 2,* edited by Elisabeth Schüssler Fiorenza et al., 237–49.

Osiek, Carolyn, and David L. Balch. *Families in the New Testament World: Households and House Churches.* The Family, Religion, and Culture. Louisville: Westminster John Knox Press, 1997.

Pagels, Elaine. "Paul and Women: A Response to a Recent Discussion." *JAAR* 42 (1974): 538–49.

Patte, Daniel. *Paul's Faith and the Power of the Gospel: A Structural Introduction to the Pauline Letters.* Philadelphia: Fortress Press, 1983.

Pauw, Amy Plantinga. "The Word Is Near You: A Feminist Conversation with Lindbeck." *Theology Today* 50 (April 1993): 45–55.

Perkins, Pheme. "1 Thessalonians." In *Women's Bible Commentary,* edited by Carol A. Newsom and Sharon H. Ringe, 440–41.

_____."Philemon." In *Women's Bible Commentary,* edited by Carol A. Newsom and Sharon H. Ringe, 453–54.

_____. "Philippians." In *Women's Bible Commentary,* edited by Carol A. Newsom and Sharon H. Ringe, 433–36.

Perriman, Andrew. *Speaking of Women: Interpreting Paul.* Leicester, Eng.: Apollos, 1998.

Polaski, Sandra Hack. *Paul and the Discourse of Power.* Sheffield: Sheffield Academic Press, 1999.

Pomeroy, Sarah B. *Goddesses, Whores, Wives, and Slaves: Women in Classical Antiquity.* New York: Schocken Books, 1975.

Portefaix, Lilian. *Sisters Rejoice: Paul's Letter to the Philippians and Luke-Acts as Seen by First-Century Philippian Women.* Stockholm: Almqvist & Wiksell International, 1988.

Robbins, Vernon K. *The Tapestry of Early Christian Discourse: Rhetoric, Society and Ideology.* London: Routledge, 1996.

Roetzel, Calvin J. *The Letters of Paul: Conversations in Context.* 4th ed. Louisville: Westminster John Knox Press, 1998.

Ruether, Rosemary Radford. *Sexism and God-Talk: Toward a Feminist Theology.* Boston: Beacon Press, 1983.

Russell, Letty M., ed. *Feminist Interpretation of the Bible.* Philadelphia: Westminster Press, 1985.

Sakenfeld, Katharine Doob. "Feminist Uses of Biblical Materials." In *Feminist Interpretation of the Bible,* edited by Letty M. Russell, 55–64.

Sanders, E. P. *Jewish Law from Jesus to the Mishnah: Five Studies.* London: SCM Press; Philadelphia: Trinity Press International, 1990.

_____. *Judaism: Practice and Belief, 63 BCE—66 CE.* Philadelphia: Trinity Press International, 1992.

_____. *Paul.* Past Masters. Oxford: Oxford Univ. Press, 1991.

_____. *Paul, the Law, and the Jewish People.* Philadelphia: Fortress Press, 1983.

Saunders, Ross. *Outrageous Women, Outrageous God: Women in the First Two Generations of Christianity.* Alexandria, Australia: E. J. Dwyer, 1996.

Schottroff, Luise. "A Feminist Hermeneutic of 1 Corinthians." In *Escaping Eden,* edited by Harold C. Washington et al., 208–15.

_____. *Lydia's Impatient Sisters: A Feminist Social History of Early Christianity.* Translated by Barbara and Martin Rumscheidt. Louisville: Westminster John Knox Press, 1995.

Schottroff, Luise, Silvia Schroer, and Marie-Theres Wacker. *Feminist Interpretation: The Bible in Women's Perspective.* Translated by Martin and Barbara Rumscheidt. Minneapolis: Fortress Press, 1998.

Schüssler Fiorenza, Elisabeth. *In Memory of Her: A Feminist Theological Reconstruction of Christian Origins.* New York: Crossroad, 1992.

_____. *Rhetoric and Ethic: The Politics of Biblical Studies.* Minneapolis: Fortress Press, 1999.

Schüssler Fiorenza, Elisabeth, with Ann Brock and Shelly Matthews, eds. *Searching the Scriptures, Vol. 2: A Feminist Commentary.* New York: Crossroad, 1994.

Schweitzer, Albert. *The Mysticism of Paul the Apostle.* Translated by William Montgomery. New York: Henry Holt, 1931.

Scroggs, Robin. "Paul and the Eschatological Woman." *JAAR* 40 (1972): 283–303.

Segovia, Fernando F., and Mary Ann Tolbert, eds. *Teaching the Bible: The Discourses and Politics of Biblical Pedagogy.* Maryknoll, N.Y.: Orbis Books, 1998.

Setel, T. Drorah. "Feminist Insights and the Question of Method." In *Feminist Perspectives on Biblical Scholarship,* edited by Adela Yarbro Collins, 35–42.

Standhartinger, Angela. "The Origin and Intention of the Household Code in the Letter to the Colossians." *JSNT* 79 (2000): 117–30.

Stendahl, Krister. "Ancient Scripture in the Modern World." In *Scripture in the Jewish and Christian Traditions,* edited by Frederick E. Greenspahn, 202–14.

_____. *The Bible and the Role of Women: A Case Study in Hermeneutics.* Translated by Emilie T. Sander. Facet Books Biblical Series 15. Philadelphia: Fortress Press, 1966.

Sugirtharajah, R. S., ed. *The Postcolonial Bible.* The Bible and Postcolonialism 1. Sheffield: Sheffield Academic Press, 1998.

Sutter Rehmann, Luzia. "German-Language Feminist Exegesis of the Pauline Letters: A Survey." *JSNT* 79 (2000): 5–18.

_____. "To Turn the Groaning into Labor: Romans 8.22–23." In *A Feminist Companion to Paul,* edited by Amy-Jill Levine with Marianne Blickenstaff, 74–84.

Swancutt, Diana M. "'The Disease of Effemination': The Charge of Effeminacy and the Verdict of God (Romans 1:18–2:16)." In *New Testament Masculinities*, edited by Stephen D. Moore and Janice Capel Anderson, 193–234.

———. "Sexy Stoics and the Rereading of Romans 1.18–2.16." In *A Feminist Companion to Paul*, edited by Amy-Jill Levine with Marianne Blickenstaff, 42–73.

Tamez, Elsa. *The Amnesty of Grace: Justification by Faith from a Latin American Perspective*. Translated by Sharon H. Ringe. Nashville: Abingdon Press, 1993.

Tanzer, Sarah J. "Ephesians." In *Searching the Scriptures, Vol. 2,* edited by Elisabeth Schüssler Fiorenza et al., 325–48.

Thimmes, Pamela. "What Makes a Feminist Reading Feminist? Another Perspective." In *Escaping Eden,* edited by Harold C. Washington et al., 132–40.

Thistlethwaite, Susan Brooks. "Every Two Minutes: Battered Women and Feminist Interpretation." In *Feminist Interpretation of the Bible,* edited by Letty M. Russell, 96–107.

Thurston, Bonnie. *Women in the New Testament: Questions and Commentary.* Companions to the New Testament. New York: Crossroad, 1998.

Tolbert, Mary Ann. "Defining the Problem: The Bible and Feminist Hermeneutics." *Semeia* 28 (1984): 113–26.

———. "A New Teaching with Authority: A Re-evaluation of the Authority of the Bible." In *Teaching the Bible: The Discourses and Politics of Biblical Pedagogy,* edited by Fernando F. Segovia and Mary Ann Tolbert, 168–89.

———. "Reading the Bible with Authority: Feminist Interrogation of the Canon." In *Escaping Eden,* edited by Harold C. Washington et al., 141–62.

Torjesen, Karen Jo. *When Women Were Priests: Women's Leadership in the Early Church and the Scandal of Their Subordination in the Rise of Christianity.* New York: HarperSanFrancisco, 1993.

Washington, Harold C., Susan Lochrie Graham, and Pamela Thimmes, eds. *Escaping Eden: New Feminist Perspectives on the Bible.* Washington Square, N.Y.: New York Univ. Press, 1999.

Winter, S.C. "Philemon." In *Searching the Scriptures, Vol. 2,* edited by Elisabeth Schüssler Fiorenza et al., 301–12.

Wire, Antoinette Clark. *The Corinthian Women Prophets: A Reconstruction through Paul's Rhetoric.* Minneapolis: Fortress Press, 1990.

———. "1 Corinthians." In *Searching the Scriptures, Vol. 2,* edited by Elisabeth Schüssler Fiorenza et al., 153–95.

Witherington, Ben, III. "Rite and Rights for Women—Galatians 3.28." *NTS* 27 (1981): 593–604.

———. *Women and the Genesis of Christianity*. Cambridge: Cambridge Univ. Press, 1990.

Scripture Index

Subject Index

Wire, Antoinette Clark, 5, 6, 7, 48, 57

wives: expectations of, 35–36, 42, 49, 52–53, 55–57, 71, 97–100, 104, 111–13, 115; NT figures, 44–45, 53, 105. *See also* couples, married

women: leaders in churches, 5–6, 8, 13, 23–24, 43, 46, 48, 53, 105–7; married, restrictions on (*see* married women, restrictions on); metaphorical (*see* female figures, metaphorical); older, instructions to, 104–5; restrictions on, 7, 26–37, 50–51, 102–5; silence of (*see* silence, of women); unmarried (*see* virgins); worship participation of, 8, 29, 37–42, 54–59; younger, instructions to, 104–7

women readers, contemporary. *See* female readers, contemporary

women readers/hearers, ancient. *See* female readers/hearers, ancient

women's experience of marriage. *See* marriage, women's experience of

women's history, tracing. *See* history, women's, tracing

women's life-transition ceremonies. *See* life-transition ceremonies, for women

"word of the Lord," 51–52, 81

works, opposed to faith, 13

worship practices: early church, 56–58; Roman, 38–42; synagogue, 14, 27

worship, women in. *See* women, worship participation of

Y

younger women, instructions to. *See* women, younger, instructions to